Acclaim for **Retarded Isn't Stupid, Mom!** . . .

"What a wonderfully honest and moving book. Both Sandra Kaufman and Nicole should be saluted for their courage and gallantry. I recommend this book not only to any mother or father of a retarded or disabled individual, but to anyone caught up in the never-ending tugs and demands of parenthood."

Josh Greenfeld
author, **A Child Called Noah,**
A Place for Noah, A Client Called Noah

"This heartwarming story . . . will encourage other parents of children with disabilities by reminding them that they are indeed not alone. . . . It will increase public awareness of a very real problem —the misunderstanding of this disability."

Senator Tom Harkin
Chairman, Subcommittee on the Handicapped
United States Senate

"a mini blockbuster"

Impact Journal on Mental Retardation

"a powerful account of a retarded child's struggle for independence"

Instructor

"Thanks to Nicole, we will all have an improved insight into the problems encountered by mildly mentally retarded individuals living in our communities."

Association for the Care of Children's Health Network

"deals very openly and honestly with problems that face adults with mental retardation . . . an uplifting story . . . provides an insight for parents that is not always available in standard textbooks on mental retardation."

Physical & Occupational Therapy in Pediatrics

"A good 'I'm not the only one' book for any parent dealing with negative feelings towards their disabled child."

People with Special Needs

"Extraordinarily vivid and moving. Readers will not only understand what Nicole and her parents went through—they will feel it."

"Read [this book] . . . for a strong dose of reality. . . . Sandra and Nicole Kaufman's lives show that parenthood is forever; that children with disabilities are their parents' greatest teachers. . . . This book is about prevailing."

"A delight to read. . . . **Retarded Isn't Stupid, Mom!** is a rich description of how one family grappled with the challenges of parenting a mildly retarded daughter. A scholarly piece of work that subtly taps the full range of your emotions and leaves you thinking."

"It is clear that Nicole (with Mom's help!) has done a marvelous job in carving out a life for herself, and yet one can't help but feel that her life will always be a struggle in certain ways. This message is both challenging and sobering for anyone (parent or professional) whose life is touched by similar circumstances."

"Nicole is a real heroine! . . . I hope that people who have stereotypes in their mind of persons with mental retardation will read this book."

Retarded
ISN'T
Stupid, Mom!

Retarded ISN'T Stupid, Mom!

by

SANDRA Z. KAUFMAN

·P A U L·H·
BROOKES
PUBLISHING CO.

Baltimore • London • Toronto • Sydney

Paul H. Brookes Publishing Co.
Post Office Box 10624
Baltimore, MD 21285-0624

Copyright © 1988 by Paul H. Brookes Publishing Co., Inc.
All rights reserved.

Typeset by Brushwood Graphics Inc., Baltimore, Maryland.
Manufactured in the United States of America by
The Maple Press Company, York, Pennsylvania.

Lyrics on pages 198 and 199 from "Is It Really Me?" by Tom Jones &
Harvey Schmidt. Copyright © 1963 by Portfolio Music Inc. All
rights administered by Chappell & Co., Inc. International copyright
secured. All rights reserved. Used by permission.

Most of the names of places and organizations in this book are
pseudonyms, and the persons, other than the members of my family, are composites. For the sake of clarity, I have occasionally trans-
posed or combined events. Except for these minor alterations, the
narrative is a true one.

First printing, April, 1988.
Second printing, June, 1991.

Library of Congress Cataloging-in-Publication Data
Kaufman, Sandra Z., 1928–
  Retarded isn't stupid, mom!

  Bibliography: p.
  1. Kaufman, Nicole. 2. Mentally retarded children—United
States—Biography. I. Title.
HV894.K383   1988   362.1'968588'00924   [B] 87-29915
ISBN 0-933716-96-6

*"What is hardest of all? That
which you hold most simple; seeing with
your own eyes what is spread out before you. . . ."*

Goethe

Contents

Acknowledgments

Thirty to forty years ago, stereotypes about mentally retarded persons abounded. The categories used to describe them reflected these stereotypes: "moron" for persons we now refer to as mildly retarded, "idiot" for people with moderate retardation, and "imbecile" for severely or profoundly retarded individuals. In institutions, the shorthand terms of "high grade" or "low grade" were frequently substituted. People viewed all persons with mental retardation as a kind of subhuman species, incapable of human emotions like love and friendship as well as any sort of higher-level thinking. It was widely believed that if let loose in the community, these "subhumans' " lack of self-control would be menacing to society: indiscriminate sexual activity and rampant criminality would be the norm. No wonder those with mental retardation were kept in institutions.

We have come a long way since then. Today, media stars participate in the Special Olympics. Television channels regularly feature sympathetic stories about men and women who are mentally retarded. Retarded children move in and out of regular classes in their local schools, and when they grow up, some of them hold jobs in the community. Misunderstanding, prejudice, and injustices persist, but progress has been made because a lot of people—parents, professionals, and politicians—have cared and fought hard.

Two who made major contributions were George Tarjan and Robert Edgerton. I speak of them because their actions are related ultimately with bringing about the circumstances under which I was able to study my daughter Nicole.

In the 1950s, Tarjan, as the director of Pacific State Hospital in California, led the movement toward deinstitutionalization. Although he was heavily criticized at the time, he persisted in his belief that some patients did not belong in hospitals, that they were capable of holding jobs, living independently, and even marrying, and that they should be allowed to do so. The critical problem was deciding which patients to release.

Some research was available to Tarjan. It had sought to identify the factors associated with patients making a good adjustment outside the hospital. Former patients in the community had been located, and questions asked of their family members (or landlords or employers) about such matters as the retarded person's employment status, number of criminal offenses, marital status, and so on. These "facts" were then examined against other "facts" like IQ, age, and sex. Unfortunately, the critical factors associated with successful adjustment consistently proved elusive.

Robert Edgerton, a graduate student in anthropology, suggested a different approach: using the traditional methods of anthropologists—observation and the interviewing of informants, in this case the patients at the hospital—he and his associates wanted to try to understand more about mental retardation and people diagnosed as mentally retarded. With Tarjan's approval and strong support, Edgerton went to work. He observed the patients washing staff members' cars, conversed with them, and learned of a long-standing free enterprise system in effect at the hospital, complete with patient entrepreneurs who subcontracted and charged rental for their equipment. Some of the patients, it appeared, were quite capable of higher level thinking.[1]

Using the same methods, Edgerton learned that not only were the patients' cultural rules for "dating" during unsupervised periods of the day complex, they included a sexual self-control that was downright puritanical.[2] He also looked at the friendship of two profoundly retarded men, one blind and the other severely spastic and epileptic, and documented the tenderness and sharing between them.[3] These behaviors demonstrated that the patients were not only capable of higher level thinking, they were as human as the rest of us. To put it mildly, Edgerton's work contradicted prevailing stereotypes and confirmed Tarjan's belief in what was then a radical perspective.

In 1960, using the same methodological approach, Edgerton moved out into the community to see how the deinstitutionalized patients were faring. His report, *The Cloak of Competence: Stigma in the Lives of the Mentally Retarded*,[4] has since become a classic in the field of mental retardation research. Edgerton found that the former patients were leading quite conventional lives. Although their life-styles were diverse, few persons had been found guilty of breaking the law, and most were keeping their sexual practices well within the norms of the wider population. He saw, however, that they spent an inordinate amount of energy trying to pass as "normal," and that their successful adaptation to community living was due in great measure to the presence of Good Samaritans.

In 1970, Tarjan led the creation of the Mental Retardation Research Center (MRRC) at the University of California at

---

[1] Edgerton, R., Tarjan, G., & Dingman, H. (1961). Free enterprise in a captive society. *American Journal of Mental Deficiency, 66*, 35–41.

[2] Edgerton, R., & Dingman, H. (1964). Good reasons for bad supervision: "Dating" in a hospital for the mentally retarded. *The Psychiatric Quarterly Supplement, 38*, 221–233.

[3] MacAndrew, C., & Edgerton, R. (1966). On the possibility of friendship. *American Journal of Mental Deficiency, 70*, 612–621.

[4] Edgerton, R. (1967). *The cloak of competence: Stigma in the lives of the mentally retarded.* Berkeley: University of California Press.

Los Angeles. Convinced that meaningful programs for persons with mental retardation could only be developed after gaining a better understanding of their daily lives and concerns, Tarjan invited Edgerton to organize the Socio-Behavioral Research Group (SBG) in the MRRC. Since then its members have continued the ethnographically based studies that Edgerton pioneered. For each study, mentally retarded men and women are contacted and then followed for extended periods of time. The fieldworker tries to blend into his or her retarded informant's life by sharing in mundane tasks like eating meals and washing dishes, as well as participating in special occasions like weddings and family get-togethers. Sometimes crises occur; these, too, are shared. Everything that happens during the fieldworker–informant encounters is recorded in fieldnotes, which provide rich accounts of the daily events and concerns of the individuals with retardation.

My first contact with the Socio-Behavioral Research Group occurred in 1977 when I was an anthropology student enrolled in the Laboratory for Naturalistic Observation class. The professors were members of the SBG. Under their guidance, I and my fellow students learned first-hand what it was like to do ethnography. We "hung around" in social settings—club meetings, hamburger huts, dentists' offices, wherever we could gain entry—and observed human behavior. We were taught skills in seeing, relating to people on their own terms, writing fieldnotes, and analyzing data. I was fascinated by the possibilities.

After I completed the course, my contact with these inspiring teachers continued. Jim Turner allowed me to accompany him to his research setting, a sheltered workshop where he had been observing once a week for over ten years. As I watched him move about the shop being greeted by first one and then another of the workers, and listening to each of them as they told him about their lives and dreams, I learned something about the patience that is required of an ethnographer.

A year later, I was privileged to be taken on as Ronald

Gallimore and Jim Turner's research assistant in the Socio-Behavioral Research Group. When I brought up the possibility of my using my own daughter as an informant, they were enthusiastic. As the project got underway and throughout its duration, they retained their enthusiasm, advised me about my fieldwork problems, and encouraged me. After Jim left UCLA, Ron continued his support. His friendship, tough standards of scholarship, and good humor quite literally kept me going during the years it took me to complete Nicole's story. I could never have done the project without his and Jim's guidance and support.

Other persons in the Socio-Behavioral Research Group contributed to the production of Nicole's story. In the first few months after my arrival, Sharon Sabsay continually met me in the hall and asked me to reflect on my daughter: "What has changed in the way you see her since being here?" "How does that make you feel?" "Are you keeping notes?" To a great extent, it was out of these exchanges that the idea of studying Nicole arose. Gelya Frank and Lew Langness introduced me to life history research methods, and took time to answer my many questions about the issues involved in such an undertaking. Paul Koegel, Steve Daley, and Cindy Bernheimer read various versions of the manuscript; all made helpful comments, and gave me incentive to continue. Andrea Zetlin, who was studying parent–retarded child relationships, was interested and supportive, and helped by sharing her perspective. Lori Stolze made particularly useful suggestions from her viewpoint as the mother of an adult with mental retardation. Harold Levine, another of my teachers in the Naturalistic Observation Laboratory class, provided expert guidance when I first turned to making sense out of the mound of fieldnotes I had accumulated. And last but hardly least, throughout the project, Bob Edgerton has been interested and encouraging. To all of these people, I am deeply indebted.

I also thank Dorothy Smith, Pete Tourtellotte, Warren Sherlock, and Judy Bobrow, my good friends who gave me valuable advice about writing and publishing, and Regional Center professionals Mark Dubie, Joan Daniels, and Marcie Alemany, and Drs. Donald Glicklick and Leonard Lipman for the time they took out of their busy lives to give me information.

Joan Carris belongs in a special category, for without her help, Nicole's story quite simply would never have been published. My gratitude for her editorial criticism is boundless.

The members of my family deserve blue ribbons for their interest in Nicole and my efforts with her, and patience in understanding when I had to stay home and write instead of joining them for activities. My husband has not only borne the brunt of this, he has always been willing to listen when I have despaired over writing problems. His suggestions, more often than I care to admit, made the difference between despair and progress. Much gratitude also is owed my sister, Camelia Berry, who sent me boxes of the letters I wrote her during the 1950s and 1960s. They proved invaluable when I reconstructed the early years of Nicole's life.

Melissa Behm at Paul H. Brookes Publishing Co. has made publishing this book a joy. Would that all writers could be treated as well by their editors.

Finally, and most of all, I thank my daughter Nicole for her willingness to be my informant. I am grateful more than she can know for so generously allowing me into her life. A special thanks also goes to Edward Brichant for permitting me to observe him with Nicole.

About the Author

Sandra Z. Kaufman, M.A., is a Staff Research Associate in the Socio-Behavioral Research Group at the University of California-Los Angeles, a position she has held since 1979. Returning to school when her three children were ages 17, 15, and 8, she earned a B.A. degree in Anthropology in 1977 from UCLA and a master's degree in Research Methods and Evaluation in 1981.

Since earning her graduate degree, Sandra Kaufman has had her writing on the relationship between mildly retarded adults and their parents published in a professional journal and has contributed chapters to several books.

Based on two and a half years of ethnographic study, Sandra Kaufman recounts, in **Retarded Isn't Stupid, Mom!**, what her daughter has taught her about being a young woman trying to make her way in the community.

Ms. Kaufman and her husband live in Southern California. Their three children live and work nearby.

To C.M.

Prologue:
Nicole at Two

The downpour stopped as quickly as it had begun—which was typical during the rainy season—and the sun again burned down. Steam rose from the tarmac around the troop transport plane.

"Probably saw a lot of use in Korea," Matt said, eyeing the old DC-3. He shifted our two-and-a-half-year-old daughter, Nicole, from one arm to the other. Since the end of the war in 1953, five years before, troop transports had been put to more mundane purposes like carrying military families to and from the United States.

Airmen rolled out the stairs, and we fell in line to board. Nicole reached over and patted the baby in my arms. To her delight, her brother made a bubble. She laughed and clapped her hands.

The line moved quickly, and we were soon settled in our seats. The plane taxiied for the takeoff, and then lifted into the sky, taking us away from the Panama Canal Zone, and the army post that had been our home for the past three and a half years.

1

Nicole cried and cried; the many changes from her familiar routine were too much for her. Finally, however, exhaustion won out, and she fell asleep in Matt's lap.

As I covered her frail body with a blanket, I again pictured Dr. McCall and Gorgas Hospital. Shuddering, I looked out of the window and forced myself to think of other, happier things—like Los Angeles, where we would be in a few hours. Matt and I had met in Los Angeles four years ago. How serendipitous it seemed, as I looked back—me, a dancer whose world was made up of ballet studios and theaters, meeting Matt, a lieutenant teaching armored tank maneuvers in the desert. Two months later we had married.

My throat tightened. Nicole had been conceived in Los Angeles. Were events coming full circle? Were we bringing her home to die? That's what the doctor had said, wasn't it—that she might die?

I looked down at her—at the wispy blonde hair and the dainty nose and mouth—and events from the past two and a half years came tumbling back.

The spinning in my brain receded and I opened my eyes. A blinding circle of light glared down on me. I turned away. Hazy figures in white moved about nearby.

The pain is gone. This must be the delivery room. I must have delivered the baby.

"You have a little girl," one of the figures said.

A girl. How marvelous.

"Is she all right?" My words slurred from the anesthesia. It was a routine question. I had no cause to think anything would be wrong.

"We had a little trouble getting her to breathe, but she seems to be just fine," the nearest figure said from behind his white mask. I recognized him as the on-duty medical officer from the night before. "She's very small though, in spite of being full-term . . . only 4 pounds, 7 ounces."

"May I see her?" I begged. Through my myopic eyes she seemed to be lying in the drawer of a gleaming stainless steel cabinet.

"Just another second or two," he said. He completed his examination and then, lifting a bundle of white blankets, he placed her beside me. I laughed with amazement at the miracle Matt and I had created.

Slowly I worked my finger into her curled fist.

"Hi, Nicole," I whispered, for Matt and I had decided on that name months ago. She twitched and wiggled while I watched.

The doctor interrupted us. "She must go into an incubator because her birth weight is so low." He scooped her up, and handed her to a nurse who disappeared with her.

That was all right. Matt would get to see her. I drifted off to sleep thinking how pleased he would be.

Nicole and I went home three days later. I placed her in her bassinet, and then, unable to keep my hands off her, I picked her up again. Love for the tiny person that snuffled against my neck tore through me. I adored Matt, but this baby brought out something primeval.

She began to fuss. "That's all right," I said, patting her. "You can cry all you want in the daytime. Just don't cry at night. Your father works hard, and needs his sleep."

It didn't happen that way. She insisted on being fed every two hours day and night. After a week I was dragging hollow-eyed around the house. Matt quietly took on sterilizing the bottles (she slept two and a *half* hours when I stopped the breast-feeding), going to the commissary, and cooking supper.

But she gained weight. When she was a month old, we took her to Dr. McCall, the pediatrician at Gorgas hospital, for her checkup. Nicole weighed in at six pounds. I laughed I was so pleased—until I realized that the nurse, the doctor, and Matt were all noticeably sober.

"Her development will be slower than average because of her size," the doctor said. "She won't catch up until she's a year old."

That made sense. It explained why Ellen's baby, Ben, was so far ahead of Nicole. At the same age he had sat sturdily in his mother's lap and looked around. Nicole was still floppy and had to have her head supported. I was reassured.

Two months later she weighed ten pounds, could smile, and could flip herself over. She could also "talk."

"And so, young lady, what would you like to do today?" I asked, as she sat facing me on my knees. She was holding her head up nicely now.

She opened her mouth, shaped it, took a breath, and out came "Ooooooooooooooh."

"You would?"

Her eyes watered, and her face turned pink with effort. "Ooooooooh," she said, changing the intonation.

But, as the doctor had predicted, her development continued to be slow. She couldn't sit until she was eight months old. Then, when she began crawling, it seemed as if she were going to travel on all fours forever.

When at eighteen months she finally began to walk, I thought she was doing splendidly, considering her slow start, but Dr. McCall expressed concern when I took her for her appointment the following week.

"I think we ought to run some tests," he said. "She's probably just delayed, but I'd like to make certain. Bring her in for a calcium and phosphorus blood test Monday. Perhaps we're overlooking something."

I nodded silently, but my heart began hammering. *What did he mean? What could be wrong?*

The fright of the actual test was soon behind us, as Nicole and I returned on Monday, but the wait for results seemed interminable.

The following week Dr. McCall finally called. Nicole's calcium and phosphorus levels were fine.

Of course they were. There was nothing wrong with my child! Why had Dr. McCall so unfairly alarmed us?

Eventually I cooled down. At heart, I had faith in the medical profession. Those people in white coats knew what they were doing, even if they did sometimes scare me.

The blood test episode faded as Matt and I enjoyed watching Nicole try out new activities now that she could walk. She was making progress, but she seemed weary, too. Whether the climate had anything to do with it or not, I don't know, but she grew more and more listless. She lost weight. At two and a half years, she weighed only eighteen pounds. Colds and flus plagued her. In spite of a diet loaded with B-vitamins and cod-liver oil, her health was deteriorating. Matt and I watched her anxiously.

Nicole cried over everything and nothing, and wanted to be carried everywhere. Sometimes she had to be transported in our arms because she was so weak. She and I practically lived at the pediatrician's office.

One day Matt took time off from work and drove over to Gorgas Hospital with us. Dr. McCall undressed

Nicole and gently examined her, as he had done so often. I tried to look at her clinically, and was shocked to realize that except for her cheerful smile, she resembled one of the concentration camp children I'd seen in *Life* magazine—all knees and elbows.

When he was through, Nicole drooped in her father's lap. The overhead fan beat ineffectively against the heat.

"What do you see as the prognosis for Nicole?" Matt asked the doctor. Why on earth was he asking that, I wondered.

Dr. McCall paused. He looked down at his papers and then at us.

"She's mentally retarded . . . she may never advance beyond the mental age of five years," he said finally. The fan continued circling. "Nothing can be done for her," he added regretfully and then mumbled something about the retarded often having short lives.

I was caught totally unaware. *Retarded?* Our child, *retarded?* This isn't happening, I thought. I dropped into a void, plummeting, plummeting.

Escape? There was no escape.

I wanted to scream at the doctor, "How can you be so calm! You've just changed the course of our lives!"

Instead I sat numbly silent. Matt and Dr. McCall continued talking. Matt got up; then I got up. He walked out of the room, and I followed him. We reached our car, and I started out alone toward the pharmacy for Nicole's prescription.

Somewhere on the walkway the tears began to come. I fled to the car. There, in Matt's arms, all the incredulity and pity for Nicole came pouring out.

"I'm so sorry," Matt kept apologizing. "I thought you suspected. . . ." He'd known for months, he said, but he wanted to wait until the new baby was born before talking about it. Two months earlier, Nicole's baby brother David had entered our lives.

Through my tears, I looked back at Nicole playing with the window handle in the back seat, oblivious to the cruel sentence that had been passed on her. How could our precious child be doomed to grow into one of those weird unfortunates who drooled and said stupid things?

Even worse, would she ever grow up? We might lose her the next time she was sick. "The retarded often have short lives." That's what the doctor had said.

"How did you know?" I asked Matt.

"I saw how long it took her to do everything—to hold her head up, to sit, to walk. . . ."

"But that was because she was so weak and small! Yes, she was slow, but she walked and sat within what Dr. Spock says is normal."

"There were other hints something was wrong," Matt said gently. "Her feeding problems in the early months. The way she fights us if we try to cuddle her. The way she stiffens and holds her breath when I try to bounce her. . . ."

"But that's just her personality."

"Sandy, those things aren't right. I don't know what they mean, but normal babies don't act like that."

I wiped my nose with Matt's handkerchief, and looked out of the car.

"You mean you never, ever thought of retardation?" he asked.

"No." The red blossoms on the hibiscus bush were wilting in the heat. "I don't know why. Maybe it was because she was my first child." I turned to face him. "Retarded or not, we've got to keep her alive, Matt. We're going home next month, and we're going to find a doctor who will make her strong and who will help her to grow. Who knows? Maybe she isn't really retarded. Maybe when she catches up in health and size, we'll discover her mind is just fine. . . ."

"Sandy, are you okay?" Matt asked. His voice brought me back to the plane and the drone of the engines carrying us northward.

"Oh, Matt," I said, reaching for his hand. "How can we stand it? *Other* people have retarded children . . . not us." I thought of the Colonel's wife whom I'd visited right after she'd given birth to a little girl with cleft palate. "I guess we forget these things can happen," she'd said to me. "We feel we're owed a perfect child. We shouldn't expect so much. . . ."

How had *I* come to expect so much?

1

No! No! No!

After transferring to a commercial flight in Atlanta, we flew to Los Angeles. Matt's mother, Charlotte, was at the airport to greet us. Her full bandana print skirt swirling about her, she swept us into her old Studebaker, and drove us to our new quarters at Fort Howard.

"One of my physical therapist friends knows of a doctor who treats children with growth problems," she said, after we had told her of our concern about Nicole. "I can get his phone number, if you'd like."

"We can't afford civilian doctors," Matt reminded us. "Uncle Sam isn't that generous, unfortunately."

The next day Matt and I took Nicole to see the post pediatrician. His response was sympathetic but as dismal as Dr. McCall's: "I'm sorry, but there's nothing we can do."

"Can't you refer us to one of the big military hospitals?" Matt asked.

The doctor shook his head. "No," he said, "there

would be no point."

Nicole came down with the stomach flu a few days later. All that night I lay beside her feverish body supporting her limp head as the retching spasms struck. This may well be the end, I thought to myself, and I tried to prepare for it.

"Dear God," I said silently, "do what is right for this child. You know best. But if You call her now, give me the strength to bear it."

The next morning she lifted her head to take a sip of water. Matt and I relaxed. But a turning point had been reached for us. I called Charlotte, got the doctor's phone number, and made an appointment.

The following week we drove to Hollywood and found his office in an old vine-covered apartment building. Beside the doorbell was a small sign: R. READ, M.D. ENDOCRINOLOGY.

"The child definitely suffers from a glandular deficiency," the portly doctor said, after he'd examined Nicole in his converted dining room. "Under my treatment you'll see an immediate difference. She'll be healthier and put on weight and begin to grow."

A jolt of new strength poured through me. Here, finally, was *hope*.

"What do you see as the eventual prognosis?" Matt asked.

"She'll attain normal weight and height by the time she's an adult, and she'll be as resistant to illness as you or I."

"Is there any possibility your treatment will have an effect on the retardation?" I asked, holding my breath.

He folded his hands across his stomach. "We'll have to wait and see. In some cases children like this catch up, but I can't promise it."

All I heard was that a chance existed. My joy spilled over. What extraordinary luck to have found this doctor.

Nicole's treatments began that afternoon. Three times a week after that, I drove a fifty-mile round trip to his office so that she could have her injections; each day Matt and I struggled to get twenty pills and two kinds of drops, all of them in unlabeled containers, into our uncooperative child.

The expense for the therapy, none of which was covered by military medical insurance, drained Matt's salary. Occasionally it created tension between us. The worst scene was over a toy.

"Where did that come from?" Matt demanded, when he came home from work one night. Six-month-old David was running a plastic car back and forth in his playpen.

I was speechless. Matt had never spoken to me like that before.

"You can't buy toys when there isn't enough money for groceries!" he bellowed.

"It cost *ten cents*," I said, having found my voice. "Can't I even spend ten cents to buy my son a toy?"

"No!" he said, as he stormed into the bedroom.

Flare-ups like that were rare, however. We were both so committed to Dr. Read's program that I didn't buy toys, and Matt kept his worries over our financial situation to himself.

A year later, when Nicole was four, we felt our efforts had paid off. She'd grown four inches, gained four pounds, and was somewhat less devastated by illness. She was strong enough to ride a tricycle with the two- and three-year-olds in our neighborhood. Her hands were still weak, though. She was barely able to push the toaster knob down, and flushing the toilet was impossible. (Unfortunately for our water bill, her little brother could flush it easily.)

Her gains in intelligence were less evident.

"She can't be retarded," Charlotte said. "Listen to how well she talks." I listened, and my hopes rose, for her diction was clear. But her use of language lagged way behind that of other children her age. I knew I had to begin to accept the possibility that the delay was permanent.

Intellectually, I could accept it. Emotionally, I couldn't. Whenever someone even brought up the subject of retardation, my insides reacted like I was being pushed off the top of a twenty-story building.

The mother of a twelve-year-old retarded girl who lived across the street called to me one day. I'd been avoiding both of them ever since we moved into the neighborhood, because I knew the mother would assume Nicole was retarded.

"Hi," she said, as I stood in the front yard watering the grass. She crossed the street.

My heart began to pound. I trembled, and my palms and face burst with perspiration.

"Hello," I said.

She came through our gate and greeted me with a smile. "Did you know a new school is being built for the retarded near here? I thought you might like to know, because your little girl will be of school age pretty soon. Susan will be going there."

I thought I was going to faint.

"Excuse me," I said. "I hear the phone ringing." I jerked off the water and fled into the house.

"When am I going to stop this nonsense?" I asked myself, as I stood shaking by the front door. "The woman was only trying to be friendly. And what she said is true—I do have to deal with Nicole's schooling."

I continued to hide from Susan and her mother, but

when Nicole was four and a half, I mustered the nerve to contact the school district offices. They, in turn, arranged for me to meet with one of their psychologists, a carefully coiffed woman who looked as if she would remain composed through an 8.6 Richter Scale earthquake. She listened as I explained my situation, but her eyes followed overall-clad Nicole who was trying the desk drawers, reaching for pencils, and climbing on and off the chairs. David, now a husky two-year-old with bright eyes, sat in his stroller watching her, too.

"We have a classroom in one of the regular schools for what we call the 'educable retarded,' or children with IQs between 50 and 75[1]," she said, continuing to observe Nicole. "Then we have a lovely new school for the 'trainable retarded,' or children whose IQs are below 50. I'm not sure at this point where Nicole would be happiest."

"Nicole, come here," I commanded. She was scribbling on the psychologist's papers. Nicole ignored me. I got up and took her firmly by the hand, whereupon she began to throw one of her tantrums. Hanging onto her hand, I sat down again and tried to make myself heard over the tempest.

"THEN WHAT DO I DO ABOUT THE SCHOOLING?" I shouted.

"I think it would be best to give Nicole some time to mature before starting school," the imperturbable professional advised. Nicole lay on the floor, her hand still in mine, kicking and screeching in rage. "When she's six years old, we'll run some tests, and then we'll know more about her placement."

Embarrassed to the core, I thanked her and re-

---

[1] In 1973 the American Association on Mental Deficiency reduced the upper limit of retardation to 70.

treated with my children.

"Can't that mother control her own child?" was what I knew she was thinking. The truth was I couldn't. Nicole had become extremely stubborn.

Even when it was time for a bath, I could count on a scene.

"Okay, bedtime! Into the tub!" I announced.

Nicole remained on the floor, opening and closing her hand on a piece of string.

I bent over her, placed my hands under her armpits, and pulled her up. "You and David can pour with the cups and. . . ."

"No! No! No!" Hanging from my hands, she pounded the air with her feet.

"When I say it's time for your bath, you *come*," I said, as I dragged her toward the bathroom. She jerked out of my grip, and ran, screaming, into her room. A lamp and toys crashed to the floor.

Nicole acted just the same in public, too. Strangers in supermarkets commented to me, "That child needs a switch." Where did all this mutinous behavior come from? David understood the connection between my disapproval and his misbehavior. Nothing linked the two for Nicole—explaining, depriving, spanking, or sending her to her room. Why couldn't I find the key to taming her?

That summer Matt received orders to attend graduate school at the University of Arizona. Painfully we decided he would have to go alone, because Nicole had to remain with Dr. Read. Matt moved us into an old cottage in Soleado Beach, the town where Charlotte lived, and he packed his bags.

The children and I took him to the train station. David cried, but Nicole screamed and clung to her father. Her hands and arms were much stronger than they'd been a year ago, and she had to be peeled off of him. Separations always caused her incredible anxiety.

The children and I returned home to a life without Matt. My days no longer structured by his schedule, I slowed down and devoted myself to the children. When eating and dressing took two hours, I didn't care. Time ceased to have any meaning.

With me relaxed, Nicole became markedly more cooperative. She nestled against me as I read her and her brother their favorite stories, and the three of us worked together on activities like stripping the wallpaper off an old bureau. I wrote Matt that the bureau project was perfect for her—just destructive enough.

But whenever she felt pressured, the stubbornness resurfaced. One afternoon, on a day when everything possible had gone wrong, I was racing down the freeway to get to Dr. Read's before his office closed. Both children announced they had to go to the bathroom. I roared into a gas station, and ran with them into the ladies' room. A few minutes later I was dragging a howling, flailing Nicole back to the car. She was spanked en route, more to impress the bystanders than to improve her behavior, and that made her scream louder and bite herself. Finally, when the door to the car was shut with all three of us inside, I turned to Nicole, frustration overflowing, and scolded her.

"You must learn that you can't always flush the toilet. You have to share it." I could hardly believe I was saying this. "You flushed David's tinkle. He ought to get to flush yours." With Nicole continuing to rage, I put my foot on the gas and zoomed off.

Once she'd gotten her injection, I calmed down. As expected, so did she. Drifting home, I chuckled to myself. The key to keeping Nicole placid was obvious: all I had to do was move like a snail and give her all my time.

The only drawback to the key was that I was by nature a wire terrier, and I was beginning to resent being leashed to a boring midget every second of the day. Too restless to play very long with other children and too unimaginative to entertain herself, she constantly followed me—washing dishes when I did, stirring each dish I prepared, and ironing on her toy ironing board beside me. These efforts were accompanied by endlessly repetitive whines of "piece of string, piece of string, piece of string."

Nothing could compensate for the tedium of her company—not Charlotte's visits (when she could find time between her job and the management of her apartment houses), not the social calls of my neighbors, not even my pleasure in watching David's nimble mind at work. By the end of two months I was becoming catatonic: my eyes were glazed, my jaw hung slack, and I was beginning to have trouble remembering my phone number.

I was ready for Matt to come home. Luckily for me, he was equally ready to end his exile.

"I can't stand this," he said over the phone. "I wanted an army career, but it isn't worth being away from my family. What would you think if I resigned?"

"Terrific! When are you coming home?"

He rejoined us, discharge papers in hand, as soon as the semester was over. The tempo of life immediately picked up. Within a few weeks he was reporting to work at Techtron Corporation. Six months later he began attending graduate school three evenings a week.

Nicole's idyll was over. Matt's needs took priority as I reheated dinner the nights he arrived home late, typed his papers, and kept the children out of our bedroom so that he could study. We made an agreement: I would have full responsibility for the house and children until he finished his degree, and then he'd take over while I went to college.

In the meantime, my experiment in selfless mothering was over. We were too poor for me to leave the children with a baby-sitter, so I took them with me. I pulled them in a wagon as I marched against the atmospheric testing of atomic bombs. I pushed them in the stroller when I rang doorbells at election time. They went with me to museums, to church, to the homes of friends, and to the ballet studio where I practiced long abandoned skills.

I felt guilty, though. My pace was so stressful for Nicole she was ungovernable. The last thing she required was stimulation. I had to have it or go mad. What I needed was a magic formula that would keep her calm in spite of her parents' activities.

In the meantime, David's pediatrician, Dr. Bernstein, was urging me to have Nicole evaluated by the Department of Endocrinology at Clyde W. Griffeth Memorial Hospital. Dr. Bernstein was a local doctor, and in the year I had known him, I had grown to value his opinion. But I procrastinated for months. Whatever peace of mind I had about Nicole was tied to Dr. Read, and since Dr. Read had told us that his therapy was unorthodox, I was afraid the Griffeth staff would question it. Dr. Bernstein finally convinced me when he said that Griffeth Hospital had a sliding scale for payments; if Nicole were under endocrine treatment there, we'd save a great deal of money. I called for an appointment.

On the designated day I left David with Charlotte's daughter, Vicky, who lived in a neighboring town, so that he could play with his six cousins, and I drove Nicole to Griffeth. An affable young resident with red hair helped to get her settled in the outpatient playroom—the services of two child care attendants were required in doing so—and then he spirited me away to take Nicole's history.

When we returned to the playroom, the resident carried Nicole away to some inner recess of the hospital. As I watched her go, I remembered the last time I had seen her in the arms of a white-coated hospital employee.

We were in Panama, and it was when Dr. McCall had insisted on that blood test. I never did understand its significance, merely that it had something to do with her being delayed, but a lab technician disappeared with Nicole into a laboratory. I stood in the hallway, waiting, listening to Nicole whimpering. Suddenly she erupted into throat-ripping screams, each one ending in a dry rasp of painful terror. They went on and on, each one tearing my insides into shreds. I had never heard a child make sounds like that. Then they stopped. Someone emerged with a syringe full of blood. I rushed in and found the technician untying large straps that pinioned a splayed Nicole to a table. A bandage was on her throat.

"Where did you get that blood?" I demanded to know.

"From her neck," he said. "Because of her size, it was the only place we could get enough."

I grabbed Nicole, incredulous that anyone could be so barbaric.

At Griffeth, Nicole would only be examined. I knew that, but the memory of the incident in Panama made me nervous.

An hour later an intern came to get me.

"Where's Nicole?" I asked.

"She's being dressed," he said. "When the nurse finishes, she'll bring her out to the playroom."

He took me to a room where a panel of white-coated doctors faced me. I frantically searched for the comforting face of my carrot-topped resident. He was there, but in a back row. Nausea washed over me, and my heart began to race.

"Dr. Read is a quack," a pipe-smoking physician said as an opener. His remark was so shattering that my own endocrine system went berserk and the start of my menstrual period was triggered a week early. "You're wasting your money."

"But she's grown. . . ."

"She would have anyway," he said, cutting me off. "Nicole has no endocrine deficiency."

I waited, dumb, for an eternity.

"What do you suggest we do?" I asked, barely audible.

"Her mental age is three years at the chronological age of five and a half. Instead of focusing on medical solutions, you should concentrate on training for the retarded."

He continued talking, but I didn't hear him. I didn't *want* to hear him. "I see," I said. "Thank you." Turning, I crept out of the room.

Matt found me lying down when he came home from work that night. "What happened?" he asked, sitting down beside me. I told him the verdict on Dr. Read.

"What do you think? Should we stop the treatments with him?" He loosened his tie.

"If we did, I'd feel we were giving up," I said. "I know she's the size of a two-and-a-half year old, but what would have happened if she hadn't been getting the supplements? We know she's more sturdy."

He stared at the tie he'd removed. "I'm most concerned about ending the 'infection hypos.' They really seem to help when she gets sick. I wonder what the devil is in those things. Funny that he won't tell us." Matt picked a piece of lint off the tie.

"Let's carry on a while longer," he said.

Nicole and I made one more trip to Griffeth, this time to see a geneticist. Blood was taken from her arm, and examined under a powerful new microscope. Her condition was not Down syndrome (mongolism), he informed me, even though she had slightly Oriental eyes, because the extra chromosome associated with it was absent. That meant the cause of her retardation would remain unknown. Frustrating as the news was, I was delighted to hear him add that Matt's and my chances for having more healthy babies were as good as those of any other couple.

A year later, in 1962 when she was seven, Nicole was tested and admitted into the kindergarten of a regular school. The following year she entered a class for the educable mentally retarded at the same location. Each day, when she boarded the special bus that came for her, she wore one of the dresses I had made for her. Underneath it, brightly hued tights warmed her spindly legs.

The tights also covered up her sores. She enjoyed school, but getting up early and dressing under pressure were more than she could handle. She coped by digging at her arms and legs.

"Beep," went the horn of the special education bus. "Good Lord," I cried. "Is it 7:15 already?" I slammed the refrigerator door and flew into Nicole's room. She sat on the bed, clad only in her tights. They were on backwards. Her shoulders were hunched in misery, as she clawed an outstretched arm.

I grabbed her dress and threw it over her head.

"Let me do it. Let me do it," she cried.

"There's no time. The bus is here. If you'd get up when I wake you. . . ." I jammed her feet into her sneakers and began tying them. She tore into a scab on her wrist.

"I hate school," she wailed. Her arm was now

bloody.

"Beeeeeeeeeep. Beeeeeeeeeeeeep."

"Matt! Make him wait. Tell him she'll be out in a second. Nicole, stop digging at yourself. Okay, all done. GO!"

She shuffled, crying, toward the door. I scurried behind her tying her sash and pulling her blonde waves into a ponytail.

"Here's your lunch box," Matt said, escorting her to the bus. He helped her up the high step.

"Wait a minute." I came flapping out the door in my robe and slippers and pasted a Band-Aid on her raw arm.

When she found her seat, she glowered out at us. She was the tiniest child on the bus.

"Smile," I called out, as the bus started up. She managed a weak one. All Matt and I could see were two huge adult teeth with a space in between.

"Progress in learning her numbers and letters has been very slow," her teacher for the EMR class said at our first conference. My insides barely fluttered, for by then I'd accepted her handicap. The passage of time had eased some of the anguish, and President Kennedy's interest in mental retardation had helped make the condition less shameful than it had been.

"Her paintings are charming, though," the teacher continued. She was an older woman who spoke in a confident manner.

"Aren't they?" I agreed. Nicole's felt-marker and pastel creations had been arriving home periodically. Unlike her brother's scribbles, her designs were carefully executed. Brightly colored shapes, some boldly outlined, others intriguingly hazy, swirled and poised above unseen horizons.

"We're having a number of them framed," I gushed.

"How nice. Nicole is a delight in the class. She not only creates interesting works at the easel, she has lovely manners."

Wait a minute. "You mean you have no trouble with her? She isn't obstinate?"

"Oh, she was at first, but once she clearly understood the rules of the classroom, she conformed beautifully."

Rules! This must be the magic formula. I must set rules. My enthusiasm soared—until bewilderment took over. What kind of rule should I set for tantrums caused by being furious at her own incompetence? or by being made to hurry? And what sort of rule would stop her anxious digging of sores into her arms and legs? or her laughter from turning into hysteria?

"Would some counseling be helpful?" the teacher asked, sensing my dismay. Suddenly I felt thoroughly inadequate in the presence of this experienced teacher who knew how to handle my child.

"Counseling?"

"You could go to the Special Children's Clinic. Psychologists on their staff counsel parents. They'd first want to do a workup on Nicole, though—which would be a good idea in any case, because you'd have a better idea where her strengths and weaknesses lie."

Nicole, David, and I went to the clinic the following month. A young psychologist interviewed me and then went to get Nicole from the child care center where she was coloring pictures with David.

"All right, Nicole. If you'll just follow me . . . ," he said, brightly. She preferred to remain with her brother. He tried every form of persuasion in his manual. Finally he bodily removed her from her chair and carried her into the testing room. An hour or so later, they both emerged. The psychologist's hair was messed up, his tie askew, and his shirttail half out. Nicole trotted out behind him, looking none the worse for wear, and resumed her artwork next to David.

Retreating behind his desk, the psychologist smoothed his hair and briefed me about his findings: ". . . minimal cerebral palsy, no neurological damage, minimal motor defects, distorted visual perception. . . .

"Particular attention should be paid to teaching her the labels to things," he counseled. "She has difficulty associating concrete things with abstract ideas. Teach her shapes like diamond, square, circle, and so forth."

"Yes, yes, I'll try," I said. He wiped his face, and I waited expectantly for wisdom on how to cope with the behavior he'd just experienced. None was forthcoming.

"I have difficulty with her," I ventured. "She has a temper. Can you suggest anything that . . .?"

"She's negative. You need to give her love, attention, and discipline." He began closing his folder.

No more than this? No miraculous elixir? No, it appeared, this was all he had to say.

"Oh . . . I see. Yes. I'll try to do that, too," I stuttered. I gathered up Nicole and David, and slunk out of the building. Neither he nor her teacher had said I was a bad mother, but that's what I concluded. A good mother would understand how to establish "rules," and how to give my child "love, attention, and discipline."

That evening the mother of a girl in Nicole's class phoned to ask if Nicole could come play the next day. I said I'd be delighted to drive Nicole over.

When we pulled up at Andrea's house, Nicole dashed out of the car. Andrea's mother, who was quite pregnant, answered her ring.

"How does the baby come out?" Nicole was asking

her, by the time I reached the house.

"It comes out through a hole put there just for babies," I said, hoping that would satisfy her. It didn't.

"Your tummy button?"

"No," I answered.

"Where you tinkle?"

"No. A special hole."

Nicole considered. There was only one way to solve this mystery. "Can I see your bottom?" she asked Andrea's mother.

"I think it's time for milk and cookies," she said, laughing. "My name's Peggy," she told me as we walked toward the kitchen. I noticed that her hair was self-cropped in a no-time-or-money-for-hairdressers style like mine. I felt an immediate kinship.

"Mine's Sandy. Thanks for taking her questions so good-naturedly. I never know what she's going to say. She'll go up to total strangers and ask the darnedest questions."

"Andrea does the same thing," Peggy said. She reached into the refrigerator for the milk.

"Andrea?" Peggy called, as she closed the refrigerator door. "Andrea?" Peggy called louder. No response.

"Oh, nuts," she said. "Here we go again." She took a key from a kitchen drawer, went to the bathroom door, and unlocked it.

"Andrea," she said sweetly, "come out and play with Nicole." Andrea remained firmly rolled up in the shower curtain.

Peggy took a deep breath and squared her shoulders. "You go on and do your errands," she said to me. "I can handle this by myself."

"Are you sure?" I asked. Nicole was in Andrea's room methodically dropping all her hostess's toys on the floor.

"Sure. We'll be just fine."

As I walked toward the front door, I listened to the confrontation between mother and daughter. It was hauntingly familiar. Nicole had never pulled the bathroom stunt, but our daily scenes were the same. Could it be that Peggy and I were struggling with similar problems?

As I drove away, I wondered about other retarded children. Were they all difficult? I had thought mental retardation meant low intelligence, but did it imply behavior problems as well?

The more I thought about it, the more I needed to know. Finally, I turned around and drove to the local library. Books on Down syndrome children were easy to find, but nothing was available on other kinds of mentally retarded children. I was about to leave when I spotted a book on brain damaged children. After a cursory examination, I had all I could do to keep from shouting "Eureka!"

Brain damaged children, I read, are hyperactive, distractible, and perseverative—they tend to get stuck doing or saying something, and they keep repeating it over and over. *Yes, yes,* I exclaimed to myself, remembering Nicole's monotonous "piece of string, piece of string."

I read on. They find change from a familiar routine stressful, have a low frustration tolerance, and act so bizarrely at times that they resemble autistic children. I cried in recognition. They often claw their arms and legs or bite themselves, and their emotions run wild because the cortical cells that normally control them are damaged. That explained why Nicole's outbursts seemed so interminable, and why her laughter so often turned to hysteria.

I could hardly wait to tell Matt. After the children

were put to bed that night, I interrupted his studying and told him of my discoveries.

"But brain damage comes from being struck on the head, doesn't it?" he asked, turning away from his books.

"Not necessarily. Damage can be caused by lots of things. It can happen before birth, or even as the baby is being born. You can't see inside the brain, so the only way you can tell there's injury is if the child has these characteristics. Nicole does. So . . . she must be brain damaged."

"What do they mean by 'brain damage'? And how does it . . .?"

"Wait a minute. Scientists don't know much about it, and I don't really care. The important thing is that *now I know I didn't cause her bad behavior.*"

I sat down on the bed, suddenly aware of what brain damage must mean in personal terms. "Oh, Matt, just imagine how awful life must be for Nicole—held captive by all those crazy impulses inside her brain."

"Poor kid," he said, thoughtfully. "Do any of the authors say how to help these kids?"

"Yes. Be patient, stay relaxed, keep the home tranquil, stick to a routine, and don't give in to her demands—everything I have trouble doing. I have difficulty being both an angel and a first sergeant."

"Tell you what," he said. "You be the angel. I'll take care of the first sergeant." He pulled me over for a kiss. "Now how about getting out of here? I have a big exam tomorrow night."

When Peggy brought Andrea over the next week, I gave her the book I'd read. She read it, and thought that the parents in our daughters' class might appreciate being enlightened. We invited them to a meeting, told them what we'd learned, and asked them about their experiences.

As they talked, Peggy and I discovered that while some of their children were like ours, many others were so passive their parents spent all their time coaxing them. Categorizing our children, though, quickly became immaterial. More important was the discovery that each of us wasn't alone. It made the evening worth repeating in other sessions. We even organized a cooperative day camp arrangement for summer, because nothing was available for educable mentally retarded children when school was out.

The concept of brain damage was helpful. But how would it affect Nicole as she matured? The answer to that still lay ahead.

2

Is Mommy tired?

When Nicole was nine years old and looked about six, I gave birth to a chubby little girl. We named her Jill. David was crushed that yet another female had arrived, but Nicole was overjoyed. She begged constantly to be allowed to hold the baby, feed her, and diaper her, and when I let her baby-sit for brief periods of time, she was transported.

"Mothering" fit right in with the rest of her domestic interests. With a perseverance that would have pulverized granite, she inserted herself into my household activities. I knew I should be firm in the face of her demands, but it was easier to give in.

I lowered my ironing board and hovered nervously as she awkwardly clutched the hot iron and shoved it back and forth on her father's shirts. She fumbled with and broke (until we switched to plasticware) our dishes in a torrent of water that nightly drained the Los Angeles Reservoir. She made cookies, as I grudgingly read her recipe ingredients, item by item, and cleaned up the soggy flour in the drawers and the milk spilled inside the refrigerator.

Actually, whenever I had time to think about it, which was seldom, I was glad she was learning these skills. I was committed to helping her develop whatever potential she had, and no one could have missed her pride as she hung up a freshly ironed shirt, served me a Mother's Day breakfast, or took care of her baby sister.

At the same time I was saddened. She would never be able to use these abilities when she set up her own home, for she would remain with Matt and me until we died. The prospect would have depressed me except that she wanted to stay with us. Whenever we talked about David or Jill leaving home when they grew up, she grabbed one of us in panic.

"I'm never going to have to go away, am I?" she would ask with frightened eyes.

"No, dear. You'll always be here with Daddy and Mommy," we said, and she was reassured.

Matt and I wished our anxiety could be assuaged as easily. We suffered from a different kind—guilt. It was our constant companion.

"Hi!" I greeted Matt when he came home from work. He shut the door behind him and stood leaning in the doorway. Jill left her pots and pans and waddled over to grab her father around the leg.

"Up," commanded Jill.

"How was your day?" I asked. He looked tired.

"Not so good. . . ." He lifted Jill up for a quick hug and set her down again.

Nicole remained on the family room couch huddled over a knitting swatch I'd started for her. The tip of her tongue clamped firmly between her teeth, she poked a needle through a stitch, clutched both needles in one hand, whipped a strand of yarn around them with enough gusto to crank up a Model-T Ford, and then tried to pull off the new stitch. It came off—with six or eight other stitches.

"Yaaaaaaaaaaah," she screeched, furious with herself. Flinging herself off the couch, she ran to where I was and thrust the yarn and needles at me. "Fix it!"

"What happened?" I asked Matt, ignoring her. "Didn't you win the contract?"

"Fix it *now*!" insisted Nicole.

"In just a minute," I said, my attention on Matt.

"NOW! NOW! NOW!" She threw herself onto the floor and pummeled it with her heels.

Matt tried to talk over her, but his patience snapped.

"Damn it all," he exploded, grabbing her roughly by the arm and jerking her up. "Don't interrupt when your mother and father are talking!" He spanked her so hard her knees buckled. She looked up at him for a second, her eyes huge with shock, and then ran wailing to her room.

Jill whimpered with fear. Matt looked at me, dazed. "Oh, my God, I've done it again," he whispered. "Is she all right? Did I hurt her?"

He hurried after her. I left them alone for a few minutes and then followed with Jill on my hip. Nicole was on Matt's lap, her legs wrapped around his waist, her head buried in his neck.

"I'm sorry, sweetheart," he said, as he held her. "I'm so sorry. . . ."

Later that night Matt and I crept into the bedroom and clung to each other. We did that often. On that particular night, it was Matt who needed to be reassured. More often it was me. "We've got to be more patient," we always resolved, guiltily aware we would fail.

Nicole, cradled by Mom, at one week.

Leaving Panama, 1958. Two-and-a-half-year-old Nicole with her father and infant brother David.

Four-year-old fun.

Sibling affection: David, three, and Nicole, five and a half.

Sister Jill's arrival overjoyed nine-year-old Nicole.

Raft time; age ten.

We wished she would stop trying so hard. Whenever she decided to master a skill, she drove herself and everyone around her into a frenzy until she learned it.

Yet that same spirit made possible the conquering of otherwise insurmountable obstacles. At times we watched her with awe.

She was determined to learn how to swim. I took her and David to the public pool, signed them up, and sat day after day with the other mothers as we watched a tanned young Atlas bring the flailing legs and arms of his assorted pupils under control. Even Nicole developed a trim freestyle. But when the day arrived for awarding the Red Cross swimming certificates, I was worried. I knew how badly she wanted to pass, but I also knew how frail she was.

The instructor explained the test requirements to his charges, and, one by one, they executed them. After David successfully thrashed his way to a certificate, Nicole was given the go-ahead. Her arms precisely cut the water and her feet executed a tidy spot of foam as she made her way to the designated spot, turned over, lay on her back while the instructor counted to 10, rolled back over, and started toward the edge of the pool. Her arms moved more slowly this time, and her kick grew intermittent. It was obvious that she was struggling. My teeth ground and my fists clenched as I sent my energy to help her, but two feet from the edge she gave out and touched bottom. A groan went up from the sidelines. All the other mothers had been rooting for her as hard as I had.

"Next year you'll do it. You'll be stronger then," I consoled her, when I hugged her after the class. She was disappointed, but I knew by the look on her face that she'd be back the following summer.

Failure meant nothing to her when she was interested in something. She dragged me outside to hold the old two-wheel bike so she could get on it and wobble down the street. She kept all of us busy tightening her roller skates. The falls she took would have finished anyone else. Not Nicole. I took her to our pediatrician to have the cuts and abrasions cleaned, and I asked him for sedatives—not for her, for me.

"I'm just joking," I said to Dr. Bernstein, as he completed bandaging Nicole's arm. "You know I'm against the use of unnecessary drugs."

"Then why do you continue giving her all those endocrine supplements?"

He'd trapped me.

Dr. Bernstein had never been comfortable with our decision to continue with Dr. Read, and Nicole by now had been under Dr. Read's therapy for seven years. "I'll keep after you, you know, until you let me take her off them," the pediatrician said.

"The whole idea scares me. . . ."

"It would only be for two months. Then we'd run some blood tests and find out for certain whether she has an endocrine deficiency or not."

Matt and I conferred. This time we decided to follow Dr. Bernstein's advice.

Dr. Read bristled when we informed him of our decision, but he mailed Dr. Bernstein a description of the ingredients in Nicole's medications. I also signed release forms at Griffeth Hospital so that her records from there would be available. Dr. Bernstein studied all of them.

"You know those 'infection hypos' you place so much faith in?" he said when Nicole and I sat in his office two weeks later. "The reason they make her feel better is because they're 95% cortisone. Cortisone masks symptoms."

"You must be kidding."

"Once we get Nicole off them, and that barrage of other hormones, and let her own system take care of things, I think she'll do very well—as well as any other delicate child."

"I can't believe it," I said, amazed.

"Griffeth believes she will attain a normal height, but at a later age than usual," Dr. Bernstein continued, leafing through Nicole's records from the hospital. "Her sexual development is also apt to be late."

I was still shaken by the cortisone revelation. "Do you think any of it did any good?"

"Possibly—at the beginning. We'll never know."

"Mom, let's go now." Nicole kept tugging at me. "Mom. Mom. Let's go now, Mom." Adult conversation was boring as far as she was concerned.

"Yes," I said. I looked at her and thought of the mountains of applesauce gray with pulverized pills that she'd consumed and the hundreds of trips to Dr. Read's office that she'd endured. "And do you know what we're going to do? We're going to go to the toy store and you can pick out anything you want . . . well, anything that's under ten dollars. We're going to celebrate."

Nicole raced down the street to the toy store. I thanked Dr. Bernstein and walked slowly after her, appalled by the time and money and energy that had been spent. Why had we persisted against the advice of Dr. Bernstein and the doctors at Griffeth? All the little answers paled beside one big one: the treatments were tangible evidence that we were doing something to help her. Perhaps it was Matt and I, not Nicole, who needed Dr. Read to get through the past seven years.

"Nicole?" I called, when I reached the toy emporium. She shouted her location, and I found her looking at the dolls. She'd stopped in front of a creature marked down to half-price called "Poor Pitiful Pearl." Its plain face was framed by straight hair, and it wore a ragged dress and black stockings. A booklet explained that it could be turned into "Pretty Pearl" by cleaning it up, curling its hair, and changing it into its fluffy pink dress and white stockings and shoes. Nicole hugged the doll all the way home.

Matt watched her dressing it that evening, and his eyes misted. "They're two of a kind, aren't they?" he said quietly.

Nicole was aware she was different. She knew the other children played with her in her yard, but often turned her away when she went to their houses. She had also heard children make fun of her.

"What does 'retard' mean?" she had asked me one day.

I deliberately continued putting the food away. " 'Retard' is a bad way of saying 'retarded,' " I replied, offhandedly. I was going to let her take the lead in this conversation.

"Why do kids call me that?"

I stopped what I was doing. "Because you're retarded," I said, taking her face in my hands. "Being retarded is like being handicapped. You know how you've seen blind or crippled children? Well, you're handicapped like that, only it's up here, in your head. It means you have trouble thinking. It's why you have difficulty with arithmetic and reading."

She pulled away from my hands and stood looking down at the button she was twisting on her sweater. She twisted it and twisted it.

"Why do they laugh at me when they say it?" Her face jerked up in indignation, the forehead pinched above the bridge of her newly acquired glasses. "I wanta sock them."

Oh, dear Lord, what do I say now? What can I tell her that would be any good at all against this cruelty?

"Just feel sorry for them," I said. "Any kid who makes fun of blind or crippled or retarded kids isn't worth thinking twice about." I doubted that my words had done much to ease the pain of rejection and taunts.

And now, as Matt and I watched her dress Poor Pitiful Pearl, we confronted her burden one more time.

Nicole's endocrine supplements were tapered off, and she suffered no ill effects whatsoever. She continued to gain in strength, to grow taller, and to put on weight.

She also gained in social awareness.

One day she sat, dejectedly, on a kitchen chair, her lunch box at her feet. She'd gotten dressed in time for the bus . . . almost.

"Good for you. Tie your shoes, and you'll be all done," I said, as I sponged oatmeal out of Jill's hair and gave Matt a quick kiss before he started out the door.

"I can't tie them," Nicole said.

"Why not?" I asked, reaching to grab Jill's milk cup before it tipped over. "David," I shouted, "don't forget your note for the attendance office."

"'Cause I'm just a poor little retarded girl," Nicole snuffled. She began to pick at a scab.

What was this? Self-pity?

"Get those shoes tied. 'Retarded' doesn't mean 'helpless,'" I barked, as I began sopping up the spilt milk.

She tied the shoes. And she never used her handicap to play on my sympathy again.

Although her health improved, and her social understanding grew, her academic skills remained almost at a standstill. By the time she was twelve, she could do simple addition and subtraction: she made stick marks on a page and then counted them or took some away. Words on a printed page, however, continued to be enigmatic squiggles. We couldn't believe that someone with a vocabulary as extensive as hers would be unable to read at least a little. But the code remained scrambled.

Wanting desperately to be literate like her parents and brother, she wrote letters. She dictated her message; I wrote it out as clearly as possible, and she painstakingly copied it, her nose almost touching the paper, her mouth sagging open in concentration. "Dear grandma. Thank you for the apron. I love it. And that's the end. Love, Nicole."

Enviously, she watched her ten-year-old brother unload stacks of books from the library every week or so. She knew reading wasn't the only thing easy for him. He could ride a two-wheeler with no hands. He could catch fly-balls, occasionally, in Little League games. He could even play "Elephant Boogie" on the piano. To add insult to injury, he was allowed to do things forbidden to her. That was too much, and she let him know it at every opportunity.

One day David asked his grandmother Charlotte, who was helping us paint the bedroom, if he could use her new tape recorder. She showed him how to work it, and then returned to her painting. He turned it on and played an uneven "Elephant Boogie" (the easier parts went faster) for posterity. Nicole hung around listening.

"I want to sing, 'Oh beautiful for spacious skies,'" she announced, inspired.

"No."

"I wanta sing it . . . I wanta sing it . . . I wanta sing it . . ., " she chanted.

"Okay! Okay! OKAY!" agreed David, worn down.

Nicole took the mike. "Oh be-ootiful for spay-shus skies," she began, voice quavering. Her confidence grew quickly. "Ah-MUR-i-ca! Ah-MUR-i-ca!" would have carried over a full orchestra.

"And now me and David are going to sing 'Jingle Bells,' " Nicole told her radio audience.

"No we're not. Gimme the mike, Nicole." His voice was suffused with the pain of having been through scenes like this a thousand times.

Nicole, enjoying the power of her position, tightened her grip on the mike.

David jerked it away. "Okay, let's see now," he said to his radio audience. "The bases are loaded. . . . Koufax throws a high, fast one. Mays MISSES. The crowd is going wild. . . ."

"I'm going to fix *you!*" She hurled herself at the piano and began to bang on it, screeching, "Blah, blah, blah, blah, blah!" David turned off the tape recorder. He knew when he was beaten.

Nicole's relationship with Jill at this time was similarly uneven. At three, the cute baby had become another emphatic personality in the house. They had terrible fights.

Yet the children had some good moments. David vigilantly protected Nicole when they went to the beach together. He mended her bike tires, and good naturedly accepted the trouncing she gave him whenever they played the card game "Concentration." For some reason, she could remember better than he where the mates to the cards were.

Similarly, she and Jill shared secrets. I found out many years later that after I put Jill to bed in her own room, she crept across the hall to her sister's room, hid under the bed, and the two of them took in the evening programs on Nicole's television set.

The tv set was the Magic Formula. I'd finally found the miracle I'd been seeking to keep Nicole calm. It worked, too—as long as she was watching it.

Actually, there were two miracles. The other was Valium. I was mortified that I'd sunk low enough to use either one, but I was desperate.

"I can't take it any longer," I'd burst out one night a few months earlier. Hearing the agitation in my voice, Matt hurriedly shut the bedroom door for privacy.

"I can't *stand* the constant fighting with Jill and David. I'm *sick* of her overreacting to everything. . . ."

"Hey, calm down. . . ."

"Don't tell me to calm down. How would *you* like to spend every minute of your day listening to her unload her problems? How would *you* like to be interrupted all day long to read her the next recipe ingredient? How would *you* enjoy telling her she'll have to rip out her seam because she sewed the wrong pieces together, knowing full well that when you say it, she's going to scream and tear at her skin?"

"I'm sorry," he said. "I wish I could help more. In another year or two I'll be through school. . . ."

"That's too late." I grabbed a dirty sock off the bed and flung it toward the hamper. "I'm going to buy her a tv set."

Matt fought a smile.

"And," I announced, "I'm going to fill Dr. Bernstein's prescription for Valium. Electronically or chemically, that kid is going to be sedated. When she's so upset the gawk-box can't do it, she's going to get the tranquilizer."

Matt grinned. "I thought the day would never come. . . ."

"Oh, Matt," I cried, "don't make fun. I feel terrible pushing her away, condemning her to lonely hours in front of a tv set."

"Don't worry," he said. "I'm sure you'll still see a lot of her."

We thought she'd be thrilled when she received the television set on her birthday. Instead, after she tore off the wrapping papers, she looked confused and hurt. She recognized the gift for what it was—a symbol of her differentness. Jill and David would continue to have their television viewing regulated, but she would be immune. She didn't like that. She wanted to be treated like them. Yet there were advantages. Her sister and brother envied her now, and she relished the opportunity for endless viewing of "I Love Lucy" and "Bewitched."

For a few hours each day it solved the problem of keeping her entertained and tranquil. But it created a new problem that was almost worse—that of two standards, one for Nicole and another for David and Jill.

"No, you may *not* watch television."

"Why not? Nicole is."

I chased them again and again out of Nicole's room, but they found ways to sneak back in without my knowing it, as Jill told us years later.

Once a month, though, when we visited my elderly parents, I could relax my vigilance. (They had recently moved from Oklahoma to a home in San Diego.) Grandpa didn't allow *any* of the children near his magnificent color set. "I won't have the video hucksters seducing young minds in my house," he growled.

Even so, the children loved going down there. My mother treated them to the best meal they'd had since the last trip, and afterwards, agile Grandpa, still the professor he'd been before his retirement, herded them across the street and down the cliffs to the tide pools. They crouched on the smooth dark rocks while he talked about the marine life in the swirling pockets of water at their feet.

Then, when they returned to the house, this same professor launched into an account of Corporate America's latest piracies, while the children entertained themselves—David whacking a tennis ball against the garage door with Grandpa's old tennis racket, Nicole at the sink flooding the kitchen, and Jill scouring the piano bench with cleanser.

We departed at the end of the day leaving behind us a trail of sand and wet beach clothes. In spite of our depredations, my indulgent parents always welcomed us back the following month, although we did hear a murmur about the piano bench.

During the years from twelve to sixteen, Nicole grew to five feet two inches tall. She became as sturdy as the rest of us, except that she was always sicker when the family came down with flu. She passed the Red Cross swimming tests, and acquired a perfect smile— after five years of wearing braces on her teeth.

New worlds were conquered. She spent hours in the ocean, under the watchful eye of her brother, attacking the waves on her surf mat. She carried a twenty-five-pound backpack into the rainy High Sierras and gleefully heated up a supper of chili-macaroni as the rest of the family huddled miserably under a tarp. She appeared as an angel sprinkling fairy dust in a local production of *Hansel and Gretel*.

She even played shortstop on a regular girls' softball team. The speed of the play often confused her, but, to our amazement, during the final inning of the playoffs, she helped to bring in the first place trophy. Ignoring the insane screams of her family, she made such perfect split-second decisions about where to throw the ball that she assisted in all three outs.

So there were successes. But not in academic areas. In 1971, when she entered high school at age sixteen, she still couldn't read, and she recognized coins with difficulty. Her spirit remained undaunted, however. After she'd been in ninth grade for a few months, her teacher completed an evaluation form for her school file. Some years later I saw what he wrote:

> *Student's relationship with peers and adults:* Nicole is well known on campus by the entire staff of secretaries, administrators, and general student body.
> *Student's behavior in the classroom:* Nicole enjoys carrying on discussions with whoever is within shouting distance.
> *Summary of student's progress including general adjustment to school:* Nicole is adjusting and so is the school.

He commented additionally that the two students who took up most of his time were the boy who enjoyed taking apart fountain pens and breaking the ink tube all over himself, and Nicole. "Nicole is into everything," he wrote. "She says just what she thinks, and goes to great mental exertions to figure out how to be in a position to tell someone else what to do."

It might appear that Nicole had developed into a friendly, irrepressible dynamo—a bit self-directed, perhaps, but coming along well. The actuality was far bleaker.

For one thing, her social exuberance was an attempt to compensate for loneliness. She was even lonelier six months later when Matt was transferred and we moved from our home in Soleado Beach to a house in the Santa Monica Mountains. I had selected the school system carefully, but had failed to consider the social implications of a special education class whose students were drawn from a twenty-five mile radius. At first I was willing to drive fifteen miles to bring a classmate home for the afternoon, but gradually I found excuses not to. That left Nicole isolated in our hill-top housing tract. As in Soleado Beach, most of the neighboring young people who trooped through the house visiting Jill and David were kind to Nicole. Some even invited her to come along to their swimming pools. But she knew they were merely tolerating her.

In order to find companionship, she wandered the new neighborhood—and, apparently, the school grounds—just as she had the old one. Anyone, child or adult, male or female, who was pleasant to her was a target for her effusive attention. Her visits to our neighbors dismayed me, yet I did little to discourage them. I didn't have the heart. Besides, if she remained at home, *I* had to deal with her.

That was the rest of the bleak reality. I was burned out. I was sick of having to read her recipes, sick of hearing her scream with frustration when she sewed something wrong, sick of feeling guilty because I wasn't more patient. I fumed over her compulsiveness: her room looked like the county dump, except when she decided at six-month intervals to put everything away so neatly that she used a ruler to line up the socks in her drawers. I was fed up with being embarrassed in public places, of standing in the Safeway check-out line and hearing her sing out across the store, "Hey, Mom! What kind of razor blades do I use? Schlitz?" I wanted to strangle her when she watched television until 1 A.M. and couldn't get up the next morning in time for the school bus, or when she patronizingly patted me on the head and cooed, "Is Mommy tired?"

Or when she deliberately did things to bait her father.

"Nicole, put the spoon down," pleaded her father, as she drummed a spoon on the table. He was building shelves at the end of the family room.

She stared out the window while her hand continued its motion.

"Nicole!" he said, more sharply.

The staring and the drumming continued. She was too "lost" in thought to hear him.

"NICOLE!" he shouted.

She kept on, her mouth going through contortions to hide her smirking.

Matt dropped his hammer and started toward her.

She stopped. "Hm? What?" She asked, as if she had just awakened from a trance.

Most of all I resented the time it took to read "one-half cup milk" and wait while she found the measuring cup, got out the milk, asked which line was "½," overshot the cup spilling milk all over the counter, had me check to see if she'd filled it to the correct line, wiped up the milk, and asked me what the next ingredient was. So I found excuses to avoid reading recipes to her.

"I'm too busy," I said.

Things were so tense between us we communicated by knee jerk most of the time.

"Turn off that water!" I shrieked whenever she touched the faucet in the kitchen.

"Stop screaming at me!" she yelled as soon as I mentioned the word "water."

And I closed my eyes to the scenes between her and her brother or sister. Because I'd found no way to stop them, I'd given up trying.

Our home, as a result, was often a nightmare. The stress level was so high that we passed each other in the hall with Nicole digging at her arms and legs, Matt wheezing with asthma, and me scratching my hives. Matt and I looked ahead with despair to living the rest of our lives like this. Whatever successes there were, they would never be enough to compensate for everyday life at the Kaufmans.

One weekend my parents came up on the train to visit. They told me later that they were shocked. After dinner I overheard them talking in their room. My mother finally emerged and asked me to stay up with her after everyone had gone to bed. By 11:00 P.M. we were alone at the kitchen table.

"Sandra, dear," she began, taking her hands from the lap of her print dress and placing them gently over mine. I always knew she was worried when she did that. "Have you ever considered putting Nicole in a residential school?"

"You bet. Preferably at the North Pole."

"I'm serious, dear. You no longer have either the strength or the will to work with her. She has no friends. If she were in a boarding school, she'd have the attention she needs, and she'd have a social life. You could bring her home on weekends or go visit her, but during the week you and Nicole would have a rest from each other. She needs it as much as you do."

"She does? I'd forgotten about her side of it," I said, shading my eyes from the glare of the overhead light.

"Matt and David and Jill need a rest from her, too. For ten years Matt has been attending graduate school as well as working full time. He deserves to come home to a tranquil household. David and Jill need a serene mother. They're abrupt with Nicole, just the way you are, and it carries over to the way they behave with other people."

She was right. We needed the peace Nicole's absence would bring. The few occasions she'd been gone the rest of us had discovered we were actually pleasant to each other. I longed for more of that sort of time.

"I'll inquire about boarding schools," I said. "I promise."

After my parents left, I learned that such schools did exist, and on a cold March day I drove to inspect the one with the best recommendations.

Sunny Haven lay fifty miles away in a rocky part of the desert. It looked discouragingly bleak, but I told myself that a leaden sky makes any landscape look dreary.

A vivacious young teacher with a braid down her back took me through the campus and told me about the dances, hikes, bus trips, and theatrical presentations during the year. Everywhere we went, men and women from ages twelve to sixty-five, many with Down syndrome features, came up to her for hugs. I was impressed. Nicole would be fortunate to be here, I thought to myself. Here, as one of the brighter residents, she would be looked up to by her peers. How marvelous for her ego.

Yet, somehow, I knew she wouldn't see it that way. As I walked toward my car, I pictured Matt and me driving her up there with her suitcases, telling her goodbye . . . and my eyes began to smart. Driving home, I felt more torn apart with each mile that passed. At what point, I sobbed inwardly, do the needs of other family members outweigh those of the handicapped child? Is it when the child makes them cross? Is it all right to keep a handicapped or chronically ill child at home as long as the other children in the family have parental role models of kindness and patience? I didn't know. I didn't think I'd ever know. The only thing clear to me was that our family was locked into a no-win situation.

I thought of a recent afternoon when Nicole had

gone out to roam the neighborhood and returned home with a crippled child in her wagon. The girl wore heavy braces on her legs. Even with their assistance, she was unable to stand up straight. She fell repeatedly when she tried to walk. She also dropped everything Nicole handed her. I was deeply touched by Nicole's tenderness to the poor creature, because the child was not only physically, and quite possibly mentally handicapped, she was also extremely demanding.

"Lock my braces . . . unlock my braces . . . get me a glass of water . . . help me walk over there . . . pick me up," she whined at Nicole.

What about the parents of that child? She must test the very marrow of their souls, I thought to myself. Yet they were keeping her at home. Were they always charitable toward *her*? I wondered.

That night, as Matt and I washed the dishes together, I told him about Sunny Haven. Carefully masking my feelings, I described the plant, the activities, and the aura of love that permeated the place. He listened carefully and, when the dishes were done, he sat down and silently looked through the application papers. After a moment or two, he placed them on the table.

"I can't," he said huskily. "She's my daughter."

The decision had been made. Nicole would have to be placed when we died, but for now we would continue to stumble along. Matt took me into his arms. We held onto each other for a long while resolving, as we had so often over the years, to be more patient and to spend more time with her. I hoped my mother would understand.

3

Everyone is yelling at me!

In 1972, shortly before Nicole turned seventeen, I had my first conference with her teacher in the Santa Monica Mountains High School. As I approached his classroom, my guard was up. If he dared to suggest that I work with Nicole at home, I was going to walk out. I was fed up with being made to feel guilty by school professionals who had no idea what it was like to live with an unharnessed charge of electricity. The last educator I'd seen had had the nerve to recommend that since she wasn't learning to read, I could make a "pretty little box" with words in it that she "liked," words I should help her learn—like *caution, riptide,* and *poison.*

My stomach churning with remembered anger, I entered the classroom and shook hands with her teacher. He was huge—a Jolly Green Giant without the green—low-key, friendly, with lots of smiles. He launched into a speech about his teaching methods and then told me about Nicole's performance in the class. I hardly heard him because I was cued into listening for implied criticism of me. It never came.

"You know," I said, finally, "I was steeled for advice when I came in here. You haven't dispensed any."

He dropped his jolliness. "How could I?" he said, quite humbly. "I have her only five hours a day. You have her the other nineteen."

Well, now, I thought to myself.

I told him about Sunny Haven. He listened and nodded. He knew of the school. "It has an excellent reputation," he said, towering over me. "But I'm glad you chose the course you did . . . " We had begun walking around the classroom examining the different activity centers and had stopped in front of a cardboard clock he used for teaching time. "You see, I think it's quite possible that Nicole could eventually move out into the community."

My eyebrows shot up.

"I've known young people less competent than Nicole who've moved out of the parental home. In a few years I could see her in one of the new arrangements where four or five retarded adults live under the supervision of a housemother. Eventually, she might live independently."

I sat down in one of the students' chairs, my jaw agape.

He smiled, amused at my discomfiture. "I think she'll be employable, too. That's why I have her working in the school cafeteria every day. She can already recognize a fifty-cent piece and give two quarters in change."

I began to laugh. At seventeen, my daughter could barely make change for a fifty-cent piece, yet this earnest teacher was talking of her living independently?

"Where did you get all these wild ideas?" I asked, a bit testily.

"They're part of a new approach in education called

'normalization.' It grew out of the civil rights movement. At its basis is the belief that the handicapped
have the right to as normal a life as possible."

I could hardly argue with that. I'd clung to that
principle all her life. But living independently? "Let's be
realistic," I countered. "Who'll help her when she runs
into problems? Her father and I won't be around forever,
and I don't want my other children burdened with Nicole's care."

"They won't be. Regional Centers are being set up
around the state to help retarded people stay in the community. By the time Nicole graduates from high school,
there will be one nearby. She'll be assigned a counselor,
and the counselor's responsibility will be to take care of
any problem Nicole may have. Nicole will have that re-
source the rest of her life."

"But what if she can't find a job? How will she
live?"

"When she turns eighteen, she'll be eligible for SSI,
Supplemental Security Income. She'll also be entitled
to Medi-Cal."

I drove home slowly and sat down in the kitchen to
sort out this new knowledge. Matt stopped his studying
and joined me. We were tantalized by the prospect of
Nicole's becoming independent. If she could do it, Matt
and I would be able to grow old by ourselves. She'd
never have to enter the benign prison of Sunny Haven,
and she'd be able to wash dishes, cook, and iron in her
own home—like other young women.

Yet we were appalled when we thought of all she
still had to learn. She'd not only have to be able to make
change, she'd have to understand money enough to
manage it. She'd have to stop treating strangers as if
they were her friends. If the goal was employment, she
was going to have to learn to tell time, and to plan ahead

so she'd be in bed early enough to get herself up and go to work the next morning. More importantly, she'd have to be able to take pressure without exploding.

We doubted she could do it. We wondered if she even wanted to be independent. But if she was as tired of us as my mother had said, perhaps she'd enjoy living in a local residence with other young mentally retarded adults. We'd worry about total independence later. After all, there was plenty of time. She'd be in high school until she was twenty-one.

Whatever the outcome, Matt and I agreed we had arrived at a turning point. Our goal for her would now be the same as her teacher's: to become a member of mainstream society.

Luckily, Matt was almost done with his schooling and could help get Nicole ready for this giant step. He had passed all his exams. All that remained was the completion of his dissertation, a book-length description of his research.

It was about time. I was forty-four years old and still had no life of my own. Like a starving refugee poring over pictures of food, I dog-eared the course catalog of our local college, musing over what my major would be when I got there. Art history? Literature? Biology? It didn't matter. I just wanted to get started.

In January of 1974, Matt's long struggle was over. We all stood outside the university auditorium snapping pictures of him in his black robe and mortarboard. His eyes blinked with a mixture of disbelief and pride, and so did ours.

"You'll spend more time with me now, won't you?" Nicole asked him, as Charlotte, Vicky, and all of Vicky's children joined us in parading to a nearby restaurant for a celebratory lunch. An onlooker would have thought the girl attired in the camel's hair coat, brown corduroy jumper, and white knee socks was about thirteen.

"I certainly will, Nicole," he said, patting the hand she had thrust through the folds of his black sleeve. "Daddy's through studying. Now it's your mother's turn."

I had already registered for spring semester classes. When I did so, though, I had become stricken with doubts. I was embarrassed to sit in classes with students young enough to be my children. I wasn't smart enough to attend college anyway; after all, I hadn't been able to concentrate on anything more taxing than a brownie recipe for years. Besides, I was tired. I was tired fifteen minutes after I got up every morning.

When the first day of classes arrived, I refused to go. Matt pushed me out the door.

Within a month or two I was glad he'd been firm. There was another woman my age in one class, and the younger students proved to be friendly. The best discovery was that my powers of concentration and my energy increased by the square of the distance I drove from the house. By the time I got to the campus each day, I felt positively zippy. I jogged to class, backpack bouncing on my back.

Perhaps my entering school was unrelated to the change in Nicole, but the daily scenes with her grew less frequent. Somehow she had matured enough to recognize that I had needs of my own. Along with Matt and David and Jill, she tried to respect my need to study. Sometimes she helped with the workload by cooking a simple supper, but most of the time she contributed by leaving me alone. She watched television and made macrame belts and pot-hangings for next year's Christmas presents. She also took care of the children in the house across the street.

Initially, Jill was concerned about the children.

"Mom," she said, "they're real mean. The mother is nice, but her kids make fun of Nicole."

"Do they? She's never mentioned it to me." I was leaving for class and had found Jill looking through the window by the front door. She had spotted Nicole and had paused a second to watch her run home from the children's house.

Nicole burst through the doorway in her ruffled orange and pink bathing suit. She was soaking wet and in high spirits. Unexpectedly finding defenseless quarry in the entry, she bent over and shook her headful of dripping curls.

"Ni-COLE!" Jill shrieked, as she was sprayed with water. Delighted by her victim's response, Nicole whooped and continued dispensing the shower bath.

Jill, realizing her mistake, rolled her eyes toward the ceiling and waited, resigned, until her sister's mischief had run its course and Nicole had run, cackling, up the stairs.

Jill wiped her face and arms with the end of her oversized T-shirt. "I guess she figures the trade-off is worth it. No one else lets her swim in their pool everyday."

The arrangement helped to make Nicole's summer more pleasant, but even for the rest of the year she seemed more at peace with herself and her lot in life. Once or twice high school students on the bus ridiculed her enough to make her come home crying, but most of the time she seemed fairly content. Matt and I were encouraged.

We debated for some time about her eligibility for SSI and whether we should apply on her behalf. Our consciences twinged at the thought of accepting money for a daughter living comfortably at home, but someday she might need it. Fifteen hundred dollars—the checks would be cut off when her bank account reached that amount—would provide a cushion during the first few years of living on her own.

I took her to the Department of Social Security, filled out the papers, and within a few months a check arrived. We showed it to Nicole.

"Oh, goody, goody," she chirped, clowning. "I think I'll eat it." She stuck a corner in her mouth and began chewing on it.

"You'll be getting this amount of money every month," I explained, ignoring her threatened destruction of the check, "and all of it is going into a special savings account." She knew about savings accounts. She already had one for her allowances and knew the bank teller would help her fill out "the paper" whenever she wanted to take any money out.

Nicole and I went to the bank. We sat down at the bank representative's desk, and Nicole immediately became best buddies with her. I filled out the forms.

"I'm gonna get a color TV," she loudly confided to her new friend.

"Not with this money," I said, signing my name.

"Why not? The lady always gives me my money."

"Because," I replied, "you have to get my signature before you can take any money out of this account." I handed back the forms.

Nicole jumped to her feet. "That's rude!" she broadcast to everyone in the bank. "You think I don't know how to handle money? You think I'll spend it?"

You bet your buttons I do, I said to myself, as I smiled wanly at the bank representative and retreated out the door with Nicole scolding me. I felt as if a spotlight were on us.

"This money will be for something important later on," I kept telling her, over and over, as we drove home. I knew my explanation was unsatisfactory, but it was too soon to talk about her moving out.

By the time we arrived home, she seemed resigned. She returned to her macrame and her black-and-white television set and we marveled. She definitely had mellowed.

Unfortunately, the improvement was only temporary, a hiatus between storms. When Nicole was twenty, Matt transferred back to the Techtron home office, and we returned to Soleado Beach. Nicole reentered her former special education class where she renewed acquaintances with old friends, and made some new ones whom she proceeded to visit on her bicycle.

"Where are you going?"

"Shelley's."

"When are you coming back?"

"In six minutes and two hours."

"You be home by five. Tell me where the hands will be when it's five," I demanded, as I checked to see if she had her watch on.

"The big hand is at the five and the little hand is straight up and down," she recited. "No, the little hand is at the five. . . . "

"Show me," I said. She pointed to the hands and gave me the correct five o'clock reading before she took off.

I soon learned that her destination and my timetable were merely negotiations endured to get out the door. She went where she pleased and returned home when the notion took her—no matter how much we scolded or punished her.

She had always marched to her own drummer, but this kind of defiance was intolerable. I called Peggy, Andrea's mother, and exploded with exasperation. "You know what it is, don't you?" she asked, when I stopped long enough to breathe.

"No. What?"

"Adolescence."

"At age twenty?"

"Why not? Everything else in their development was delayed."

When I stopped to think about it, the symptoms were there. The long telephone calls. The whisperings to a girl friend about boys. The experiments with hairdos. The touchiness about privacy.

Even the assertions of independence. The non-retarded daughters of our friends were all at college or living on their own, and Nicole made it quite clear she intended to follow suit. "I can't wait to move out," she snapped. Matt and I didn't have to worry anymore about whether she wanted to leave home.

She insisted on doing more things for herself. Ironically, her efforts only involved us more. Especially when it came to phone calls.

The worst offenders were the attempts over the phone to relay car-pooling plans for Go-Getter events. Go-Getters was a club for developmentally disabled young adults that Nicole had joined, and the members took turns with the phone list.

One day Andrea phoned to inform Nicole of the transportation plans for a bowling party. The conversation started off amicably enough.

> Andrea: We'll come get you and then we'll get Roger.
>
> Nicole: That's dumb. (Roger lived on the other side of the highway. Bill, who lived only two blocks away, was always picked up immediately after Nicole.)
>
> Andrea: Not dumb.

Nicole: It is, too. Then you have to come clear back here to get Bill.

Andrea: (impatiently, convinced Nicole was deliberately provoking her) He's in the car!

Nicole: Now?

Andrea: (voice rising) No, stupid! Tonight!

Nicole: (confused and angry) That's impossible.

Andrea: (yelling) No it isn't!

Nicole: (yelling) Yes it is!

Nicole heard the phone slam down. She followed suit. "That's rude!" she shouted. "That's so rude!"

She marched into the kitchen and began slamming cabinet doors. I called Peggy who told me Bill's mother was driving the car pool. Andrea had assumed Nicole knew that.

Nicole and her friends were constantly leaving out critical information when they talked to one another. They also used verb tenses incorrectly and decoded messages like "Be here in ten minutes" as "We'll be there in ten minutes." As a result, parents were forever called upon to soothe ruffled tempers.

The bicycle tours and the demands that she be allowed to handle her own affairs were trivial, however, compared to the real problem Nicole's adolescence presented—her awakening sexuality. Over the years, as Matt and I had peered nervously into the future, nothing had worried us more. Morality wasn't the problem. We were terrified about pregnancy.

When her periods began at age fifteen, a friend of mine with normal children had suggested that I have her Fallopian tubes tied to ensure her sterility.

"She'd never need to know," my friend had confided.

Could parents legally do that? I'd wondered at the time. If so, the idea was tempting. Nicole would be free to enjoy sexual intimacies, and Matt and I could relax. Something in me, however, had recoiled from the idea of playing God with her fertility. I'd pushed the whole problem out of my mind.

Now that she was flirting with boys over the phone, we could no longer avoid the issue. Something would have to be done before she moved out into the community. Fortunately we had time. She wouldn't be leaving home for a number of years after high school, and during that time the social occasions would be well chaperoned Go-Getter events.

She dated while in high school on only one occasion. The young man was a classmate who took her to the prom in her senior year. (Nicole probably asked him. I wouldn't have put it past her.) Matt and I were quite impressed with her that evening. Before the dance, she and her date and two other couples, all of them resplendent in their tuxedos and formal gowns, enjoyed a candlelight dinner prepared by Nicole—steak, baked potatoes, salad, and strawberries in cream. As she went out the gate, she looked like sweet sixteen, slim and stylish in her empire-style long dress, her $1200 smile, and her blonde hair swept up in curls on top of her head.

We didn't hear much about the dance, but we think she had a good time. Many years later a color photograph fell out of her scrapbook. In it were Nicole and her date in front of a poster-painted palm tree and sunset. She was seated on his lap, her hands clamped on either side of his head while she planted a kiss on his surprised face.

She remained in high school until a few days before her twenty first birthday in June, 1976. To her disappointment, she had to miss her own graduation in order to attend her brother's at Greenfield Academy in Massachusetts where he'd been a student during his junior and senior years. The entire family traveled east for that event. Nicole now thought of David, at eighteen years a lanky six-footer with a deep voice, as her big brother. She looked up to him, both figuratively and literally. Sniping continued between her and twelve-year-old Jill, but the fights with David were over.

As compensation for missing her own graduation and as a birthday treat, Matt and I took Nicole to Disneyland, her favorite recreational spot, when we returned to California. She brought along a boy named Edward who, she said, had been "nice" to her in high school. He'd been in the Educationally Handicapped classroom right next to hers, and every day after lunch they'd chatted while standing in their respective lines waiting for the classrooms to be opened.

We drove inland to the next town to pick Edward up from his apartment where he lived with his mother and two brothers. He was a slight lad with dark features— French Canadian, he told us on one of the few occasions during the day when he found the courage to speak. He also revealed that he was nineteen and a new graduate like Nicole. We saw little of him, however. Or of Nicole. She grabbed him by the hand and hustled him from one Disney attraction to another, stopping only briefly when she checked in with us every two hours at the patio restaurant where Matt and I sat drinking iced tea and reading.

"I just *love* 'It's a Small, Small World'," she squealed, when they joined us for a quick hamburger. "It's a small world after all, it's a small world after all . . . ," she sang and then burst into laughter. The ride through the fantasy of animated dolls from around the world had always been her favorite.

Edward ignored her. He was more interested in the distant Matterhorn where shrieking passengers were plunging in and out of tunnels on their downward course. From where we sat the mountain looked like it was made of *papier maché.*

"You want to go on the Matterhorn again?" Nicole asked him, as she munched on some of his french fries.

"Yeah," he mumbled.

"Okay, we'll do that after 'Pirates of the Caribbean.' " Edward ate slowly and finished only three-fourths of his food. As soon as possible, Nicole whisked him away.

Matt refilled my iced tea glass and I went back to my studying. I was always studying. I was so addicted to it, I'd signed up for summer school.

"Anthropology again, I see," Matt commented, glancing down at my reading material as he adjusted the umbrella over our table.

"Margaret Mead writing about her fieldwork in New Guinea." I showed him the cover of my paperback. "Listen to this. She discovered that the Papuans. . . . "

Matt began to chuckle. "That's what's so great about having a major in anthropology. It's so practical. Employers will be falling all over themselves offering you jobs after you get your degree."

"You be nice to me," I sniffed. "I can't help it if I'm fascinated by the idea of studying people in an effort to see the world from their point of view. That's what Margaret Mead did, and that's what I'm going to do one day. Somewhere. Somehow. You'll see."

Matt sat down. "I hope you can, if that's what you want," he said, chastened by my earnestness. "I just hope you'll do it a little nearer home than Margaret Mead did."

We watched Nicole and Edward making their way

toward us through the crowded tables. Both were grinning. Black caps with big Mickey Mouse ears rode on their heads.

"What do you think of Edward?" Matt asked.

"I'd like to scrub his dirty nails and teeth, but other than that, he's rather sweet. They seem to be good friends."

"Daddy!" Nicole shouted. Everyone within fifty feet turned to look. Oblivious to their stares, she burst into raucous laughter, delighting in how she was shocking us with the outrageous ears. By the time she reached our table, her amusement was out of control. She was hysterical.

"Stop it," commanded Matt. The laughter continued. "Nicole, stop it," I said, firmly. Her body shook, and the sound disappeared. Her eyes pleaded like those of a drowning woman.

I slapped her across the face. Stunned, she dropped into a chair. The shocked stares of onlookers burned into me.

I held tight to her hand as the sound returned, and then as the uncontrolled giggles gradually died down. Edward stared at her curiously.

"I'm sorry," she said, squelching a last bubble of mirth. "I couldn't help it."

"It's okay, sweetheart. I'm sorry I slapped you."

We all sat silently until she was completely calm. Matt checked where she and Edward were headed next and whether they had enough money, and off they went, Edward shuffling along behind Nicole as they wound their way through the tables. Slowly people's attention returned to their own affairs.

"I'm drained, absolutely drained," I said. "She's always had trouble putting a lid on her emotions, but I thought it was getting better."

"It is. Just a few years ago, she was so excited she threw up all the way to Disneyland and kept it up after she got here. She doesn't do that anymore."

I stared, unseeing, at a toddler trying to take a picture of his amused parents. "Was I wrong in slapping her?"

Matt looked down at his iced tea. "What's done is done. I don't know what else would have stopped her."

After that day, the frequency of phone calls between Nicole and Edward increased exponentially. When I saw her pulling the phone into her room and closing the door, I decided the relationship wasn't as platonic as I'd thought. I began to be grateful that he lived a good five miles away with enough hills in between his home and ours to deter even the most resolute cyclist.

The summer of 1976 was noteworthy for more than the introduction of a romantic interest in Nicole's life. In August she joined the work force.

It happened because she'd met a new benefactor. She'd known a number of them during her life, people who gave of themselves so unstintingly on her behalf they can only be described as saints. One was the cafeteria supervisor who had worked with her at Santa Monica Mountains High School. Month after month, she had patiently taught Nicole how to tell the difference between a fifty-cent piece and a quarter, and how to carry out tasks in a busy kitchen without becoming unglued.

Daniel Gold was her new benefactor. He was the grandfather of the cafeteria supervisor, and he offered to hire Nicole part-time in his restaurant as well as train her. Daniel Gold was handicapped, too. His larynx had been removed a few years before.

Nicole donned the prescribed blue tunic with red

sailor tie, poked her hair into a net, and showed up at The Chowder Bowl, one of the fast-food emporiums near the fishing pier. She was soon doing battle with a line of toasters, a grill, three deep fryers—and Mr. Gold. He was a man of powerful wrath, and he quickly discovered he'd met his match with Nicole. Her ineptitude and temper tried his patience sorely. Shaking with a rage he couldn't vocalize, he wrote her notes—which she couldn't read.

"Two burgers one hold the onions," shouted a waitress. The day was hot and business brisk. Crowds of hungry customers pressed against the front of the forty-foot long counter. On the other side of it, uniformed employees flew back and forth rescuing shakes from the whirring malt machines, jerking Cokes from the Coke dispenser, spearing ears of corn from the steamer, and ladling bowls of clam chowder. Every few seconds one of the cash registers clanged.

In the middle of it all, standing with her back to the customers and her feet planted like the supports to the San Francisco Bay Bridge, was Nicole. She squinted in the direction of the waitress and went back to dribbling pickles on a line of paper plates. A few fell on the floor. In front of her a half dozen hamburger patties shriveled on the grill.

Daniel Gold hung up the phone. He sped toward her, jerked up a basket of sputtering brown sticks that used to be french fries, and stabbed his finger at the timer.

"I *set* the timer!" she lied. Dismissing her answer with a wave of his hand, he dumped the brown sticks into the trash. That done, he slapped the hamburgers onto the paper plates.

Perspiring profusely, his mouth exaggeratedly shaping a soundless "two," he held up two fingers, shook them at her, and pointed toward the pickle container with his other hand.

"There isn't time to count out two," she shrieked.

Daniel Gold turned purple enough to self-destruct. Wheeling, he charged into his office. Smoke began rising from the toasters.

"Ham and cheese on wheat," belted out another waitress. Nicole was too busy throwing away burned buns to hear her.

Daniel Gold reappeared, scribbling on a pad of paper which he thrust at Nicole.

"I have *told* you and *told* you," it said. "Either you put *two* pickles on the plates, or you're fired."

His note looked like chicken scratches to her.

"Nicole! Where's my burgers?" called the first waitress.

"Everyone is yelling at me!" screamed Nicole, clapping her hands over her ears. A fryer timer started ringing, and Mr. Gold gesticulated wildly in its direction.

Fortunately, there were people we could call on for help. As soon as Mr. Gold had offered Nicole the job, I had signed Nicole up at the new Regional Center near us, and a spirited young counselor named Gordon Wade now jumped in to adjudicate. He also mobilized the people at the Department of Rehabilitation. Matt and I were grateful to everyone for trying so hard.

We were determined that she keep this job. Gordon explained that the decision carried hazards: her eligibility for SSI would be cut off after nine months' employment, and reinstatement would be difficult, if not impossible, from then on. Although that was a scary proposition, we opted for the wage earning. It was more "normal" than receiving government checks.

Nicole was delighted with Gordon. She called him every day to tell him her problems. The content of their discussions remained confidential, but Gordon told us that she firmly resisted all efforts to lure her into attending classes designed to teach mentally retarded young people "independent living skills." She was already getting too much of that kind of training at home, thank you.

Everyday Matt struggled to instruct her in things like using a bus, taking responsibility for getting herself to work each day, and planning ahead so that her uniform would be washed. He also tried to teach her how to budget her money.

"Where are your receipts?" he asked as they sat in her room.

"I don't know," Nicole giggled.

"How much money do you have left?"

"I can't remember."

"Where is your purse?"

"I'll find it in a minute," she said, sobering because her father was getting angry. She began to paw through the debris on her bed.

"Where is your paycheck?" Matt's voice rose in exasperation.

Her voice rose, too. "I put it somewhere."

She eventually found her purse and Matt counted the money. She was sixteen dollars short. "You're irresponsible," he scolded. "You can't live alone and behave like this. You won't have enough money to eat. Your money just disappears."

Silence.

"Grandma Charlotte owes me a dollar," Nicole offered tentatively.

Silence.

"Oh, I know where it is," she burst out, revealing how little she understood of the task at hand. "I got paid six dollars for baby-sitting."

"Then that's six dollars *more* you can't account for."

"No. No. You don't understand. I got six dollars *extra!*"

I was impressed by Matt's patience. I had lost mine long ago.

"I want to leave home," Nicole announced daily.

"Fine. As soon as you prove you're capable of handling your own affairs, you can go."

"I want to move out *now*. I know what it's like to live on your own. Edward tells me."

"Edward lives with his mother," we countered, incredulous at her reasoning.

We soon discovered she was using her new bus expertise to go to Edward's. Even when she was supposed to be at The Chowder Bowl, she took a detour to his home. She was also giving him money.

Her deliberate sabotaging of Matt's training program was bad enough, but her offhand attitude toward me made me apoplectic. Often, after I had been wild with worry for hours because I had no idea where she was, she'd saunter in and flippantly inquire, "Hi, Momsy. Did you have a nice day?" When I demanded to know where she'd been, she lied. Yet she expected me to save dinner for her, do her laundry (she never had "time" to do her uniform), scrub the pots and pans although they were her job, take her phone messages, and chauffeur her to Go-Getter meetings.

"I can't take it any longer," I fumed to Gordon. "She pushes me in the mud and then walks on me. I won't put up with it."

"You can't afford pride," he cautioned. "She'll leave, and you may never see her again."

I gulped and returned to the pots and pans.

"I know. We'll redecorate her room as a surprise for her twenty-second birthday," I told Matt, after enduring a year of Nicole's indignities. "She'll love it so much she'll want to stay home, and then we'll have more control over her."

He was willing to try anything I suggested. While she was at camp for a week in June, he stained unfinished furniture and painted wicker chairs, and I sewed. We were delighted with the transformation. Nicole had a charming teenager's bedroom complete with couch bed and pillows, desk, pretty curtains, a window ledge for plants—even a decorative shelf for her treasured knickknacks.

She seemed pleased when she came home. "Where'd you get the pillows?" she asked, examining the eyelet edging on one of them.

"I made them," I clucked.

"Really? They're cute."

Matt and I crossed our fingers.

Within a month she was mumbling about wanting to buy a "bedroom set" from Edward's brother—a double bed, huge dresser, and equally large mirror that sat on top of it.

"It's only sixty or forty dollars," she said airily.

"Nicole," I said, "you already have new furniture. You do not have sixty or forty dollars. Your room is too small for furniture of that size."

She fixed me with a look I had long since learned to dread.

"You will not," I stated with great emphasis, "I repeat, *not* purchase that bedroom set. Do you hear me?"

She turned and clumped upstairs to her room.

In August, Matt and I went to Europe for a month with Charlotte and Jill. David, who was working and attending summer school at UCLA, moved back into the house from the apartment he'd been sharing with a friend so that he could keep watch on Nicole. He knew it was going to be a challenge, and he wasn't disappointed.

For a few days he kept brief notes of her activities:

Saturday: Got home from work, found Edward in Nicole's room. Nicole had bathrobe on. Lecture.

Sunday: Got home at 11:30 P.M. Edward in Nicole's room. He'd "missed" the bus. Nicole wanted him to spend the night. No way. I took him home.

Monday: Nicole home from Edward's at 11 P.M. instead of 10 P.M. like I'd told her. "The movie got out late," she said. / Discovered she stole $2 in change from my room. Lecture. / She blew all her paycheck in one day and wouldn't tell me where it went.

Tuesday: Nicole sick. Thank God.

Wednesday: I was at my apartment for the night. I think Edward spent night with Nicole but no way to prove it.

Thursday: Nicole spent day moving enormous bed and dresser and mirror into her room. Have no idea where her own furniture is.

David was overjoyed to have us come home. Nicole had her doubts. I took one look at her room and broke out in hives.

"Surely other parents are going through these same problems," I said to Matt, as I scratched my hives. "Let's go to some of the parent meetings. Maybe we can learn something."

For a while we resumed attendance at the Go-Getters parent group sessions, but the discussion invariably centered on how to teach reluctant sons and daughters to cook and iron and do laundry. No help there.

Meanwhile, Nicole was coming and going at all hours of the night. Some nights she failed to come home at all.

Matt and I were frantic. Worries about her holding onto her job and saving money were forgotten as we stewed over her being knifed on street corners while waiting for buses at 2 A.M. The nightmare, though, was pregnancy. I was damned if I were going to be straddled with her children. I marched her off to my gynecologist, and the two of us did our best to present a tubal ligation in a favorable light.

"But I like babies," Nicole whimpered, when she understood that it permanently ended the possibility of having children. "I want to have a baby. They're so cute and cuddly." I clutched my purse, torn between pity for her and my own desperation.

The doctor began to explain the various birth control methods. Nicole's eyes glazed, and she yawned. It was useless to continue. I was certain she couldn't be trusted to use any of them anyway.

Gordon, meanwhile, was working around the clock to convince Nicole that she was hurtling toward disaster—to similarly little effect. He arranged for weekly sessions at our home with a budgeting counselor. Nicole didn't show up. He came at 7:30 A.M. to personally escort her to a birth control clinic. Nicole couldn't be found. The only success he'd had was that so far he'd convinced Daniel Gold to keep her on at his restaurant.

One evening she showed up at home, a huge plastic garbage bag slung over her shoulder, just as we were finishing dinner. As soon as she came in the door, Matt and I began the nightly grilling.

"Why are you so late? Where have you been? You were due home at seven. What were you doing?"

She dropped down on the stairs, legs sprawling, and leaned against the railing. Her knee socks were rolled down into fat doughnuts above her sneakers, just the way she liked them. Emblazoned across the front of her tight new T-shirt was the announcement "Looking's Free. Touching Costs."

"I had to wait two hours for the bus . . . or maybe it was fifteen minutes."

"What's in the sack?"

"Stuff," she stated enigmatically, ending further disclosure.

"You realize you'll be punished," her father warned her.

"I'm moving out," she said.

"You're what?"

"I'm moving out." Her almond eyes sparkled in defiance.

"I'm over twenty-one. I talked to a policeman and he said you can't stop me, and I paid the lady sixty-five."

Matt and I put our forks down carefully.

"What lady?"

"The apartment lady."

"Where? What apartment?"

"On the street where the bus turns. The lady wrote it down." She produced a rumpled scrap of paper with an address on it.

"You can't possibly rent an apartment," I sputtered. "You don't have the money necessary for the cleaning fee and the first month's rent and . . . "

"Yes, I do. I'll get it out of that bank account where those checks are. You said they were for later."

Why, you cagey little imp, I thought. *You don't miss a trick.* "Yes, that money is intended for when you move out. But you're not ready," I exclaimed. "You're still not on birth control. You still blow your paycheck as soon as you get it. You wander the night at all hours." I had the feeling I was talking to myself. "You show up at work when you feel like it. You don't eat properly unless I fix your meals . . . "

"If you insist on going," Matt interjected, "let us at least find you an apartment nearer us. This one is half an hour away."

"No, I like this place. I found it myself."

Matt and I knew it was useless to argue with her.

The following Sunday we loaded the bedroom set onto a truck and drove inland to the address she gave us. She said she would meet us there after taking the bus from work.

The neighborhood was an older one full of small apartment houses. We pulled into a pot-holed concrete driveway at the proper address, and Nicole came tearing around the corner of a faded stucco building.

"In here, Daddy. In here!" she squealed.

"Calm down, Nicole," he said, afraid she'd become hysterical again.

With her frenzied directions we carried everything into the dingy room she had rented on the ground floor. I showed her how to work the ancient stove and, with great disquiet, helped her make the double bed. Edward stood silently watching us.

"Now, promise me you won't let anyone into your apartment, ok? And you'll always keep the door locked?"

"I will, Momma," she said.

It was time to go. I lingered a moment while I arranged in a jelly glass a few flowers I'd brought from our garden. As I placed them on the kitchen counter, I thought of the pediatrician in the Panama Canal Zone. His words were as clear to me then as they'd been the day he'd said them twenty years before.

"She may never advance beyond the mental age of five years." His prognosis had been accurate. Nicole's latest California Achievement Test scores placed her at the first grade level. Yet here she was trying to live on her own. I wondered if psychologists had a way to measure *chutzpah.*

We walked out to the truck, she and I, our arms around each other.

"You'll call me tomorrow?" she asked. The old anxiety at partings was still there. "But don't come over until I invite you," she warned, before I could answer.

I kissed her forehead. Matt and I got into the truck. As he backed it down the driveway and carefully rejoined the traffic, we got our last glimpse of Nicole, waving, as she stood by the entrance to her new home. Edward was beside her.

"Do you suppose," I mused to Matt, "that the troubles will begin tonight or tomorrow?"

"Maybe she can make it 'til tomorrow," he said.

The first call came the next morning. She had seen a roach. That night she couldn't find her bus pass. The next morning she called in alarm because she smelled gas coming from somewhere.

"Is the pilot on in the oven?" I asked.

"What's the pilot?"

"Remember the little flame I showed you at the back of the broiler? See if it's lighted."

"Just a minute. I'll look."

I waited. And waited. Had she passed out? So much time passed I began flipping through the phone book for emergency numbers. Then I heard the toilet flush.

"Sorry," she said, "I had to go. Yeah, the little flame is there."

"You still smell gas?"

"Yeah. It's real bad."

"Go find the landlady and. . . . "

"Okay. Wait a minute. . . . "

"NICOLE!"

"What?"

"Hang up *first* and call me back."

The following day she burned her hand. And so it went. Our house was blissfully quiet with her being gone, but my work load had doubled. Now her phone calls interrupted whatever I was doing, and I had to drive eighteen miles each way to rescue her.

Meanwhile, she made no effort to go to a birth control clinic, to control her money, or to go to work faithfully. When I discovered that Edward had moved in with her, I blew up.

"She barely makes enough money to support herself," I squawked at Matt. "He has normal intelligence. Why doesn't he get a job?"

The next day I was studying for exams when she called about a money crisis with her landlady. I raced over there, straightened things out with the landlady, stamped back to Nicole's apartment, and spun to face her. Edward scurried into the bathroom.

"Look, Nicole. I'm sick of your problems. I told you you weren't ready to move out, but you insisted. We asked you to move closer, and you refused. Okay. You've made your bed. Now you lie in it." As soon as the words left my mouth, I knew I was in trouble.

"My bed isn't made," she said, her face a mass of confusion as she looked at the rumple of sheets and blankets.

I wanted to beat my head on the wall and weep.

After six months, she relented, and we installed her (and Edward) in an old duplex belonging to Charlotte. Now the travel time was only six minutes. The scenes between us continued, no matter what her address.

Every time I saw her, I launched into a tirade. "Why

didn't you get a receipt? When are you going to the birth control clinic? Are you or aren't you going to work tomorrow? When are you going to wash these filthy dishes? No wonder you're getting fat. Look at what you've got in this cupboard—junk food."

She spat back answers. "I lost the receipt. I'll go to the clinic next week. I was sick last Friday. I ran out of dish detergent. All Edward likes to eat is Twinkies and potato chips."

Gradually she called less often, until I heard from her so seldom that I began calling her. She was distant. She had no interest in hearing from me.

"At last," I sighed to Matt. "We're rid of her."

All Nicole spelled for me was TROUBLE. Let her ruin her life. I had no intention of picking up the pieces.

4

I **am** capable.

I was finally free to get on with my life. After transferring to the University of California, I practically lived in the anthropology department for the next year and a half.

Sometimes, when I crossed campus, I ran into David. His description of poverty was always so convincing, I'd treat him to lunch—providing he let me peek at the latest architecture designs in his portfolio.

Being with David—or Jill—was always fun. Oh, they worried me, and I fussed at them from time to time, but watching them grow was rewarding. Whenever classmates asked if I had any children, I was eager to talk about them.

"Here's a picture of David," I'd say, producing photographs. "He's here at UCLA. And this one who looks like she's choking the dog is Jill. She's fourteen and can't wait 'til she gets the braces off her teeth."

The photos were duly inspected, and I waited for the inevitable next question. "You have just the two?"

"No," I'd say, putting the billfold away. "I have a retarded, older daughter. I don't have a picture of her."

"Oh." (Pity in the voice.) "Does she live at home?"

"No. She lives in her own apartment."

"Really?" (Great interest in the voice.)

"How did you answer question three on the exam?" I'd ask, changing the subject. I had no intention of disrupting my serenity by discussing Nicole. UCLA was my escape from all that.

But not for long.

"One of my professors is looking for a research assistant," I told Jill and Matt one night, shortly after I received my bachelor's degree.

"You're going to apply, aren't you?" Matt asked, looking up from his book on citrus production. He had begun buying orange groves in the San Joaquin Valley, and each evening he studied up on the citrus industry.

"I don't know. If he hired me, I might not get to do field work right away, but I would eventually, and it would be right here in Los Angeles. That's the good part."

"What's the bad part?" asked Jill.

"The professor is studying mentally retarded adults living in the community." The thought thoroughly dismayed me. I'd had twenty-three years of mental retardation and didn't need another minute.

"Apply anyway," Matt said, without hesitating. "You may be in a rocking chair by the time the next job in anthropology shows up."

I filled out the application forms. When I learned I'd been accepted, my feelings were mixed. I found myself tucked into a corner of the Mental Retardation Research Center doing desk work, as field workers hurried by me on their way to final visits with their "informants," the men and women they were studying. The two-year research project, I discovered, not only was ending, it might be years before a new one was funded. That finished any hope of doing field observations for some time to come.

As I sat at my desk stewing over my disappointment, Nicole called. I was surprised to hear from her, but I knew what she wanted.

"No, Nicole," I said, "I'm not going to let you have the rest of the money in that savings account so you can buy a moped."

"Why?"

"I've already told you. Even though it seems like all the other young people in town have mopeds, you don't have the judgment to ride one. Also, it's illegal to ride one without a driver's license, and you can't get one because you'd have to be able to read the vehicle code and understand it to be able to pass the test."

"Jill rides her moped without a license," Nicole flung back at me.

The last thing I needed in my frame of mind was an impudent daughter pointing out my inconsistencies.

"I have work to do. I have to get off the phone," I growled and hung up.

I slumped forward, elbows on my desk, forehead in the heels of my hands. To add to my disappointment over being unable to do field work, I was sick with guilt and sadness about Nicole. All around me I saw the friendships that had grown up between the field workers and their informants. Nicole had no such friend in me. In the year and a half since she'd left home, she'd moved further and further out of my life. I didn't want to lose her. Yet whenever we spoke, we were combatants, and I saw no way of breaking the pattern.

Maybe what I should do is take Nicole on as an informant, I joked to myself. Then we, too, could be friends. The more I thought about it, the more seriously I considered the idea. Why not? My mind whirled with the possibilities. I'd get to do field work after all. Nicole would be my special project.

But could I suddenly become neutral? A field worker has to be. Could I remain scientifically detached if I learned she was staying home from work day after day? Or if she told me she was pregnant? Could I sit back and watch her non-judgmentally if I discovered she was stealing or taking drugs? No. Impossible.

Then I thought of the material waiting to be collected. Nicole could tell me about her life, and I would compile it in her words. Why, it would be unique. I could just see it in print: "Autobiography of a Handicapped Daughter." How Nicole would love that. As a neophyte professional eager to become published, so would I.

That settled it. My desk work was forgotten for the remainder of the afternoon as I plotted how and when I would approach her.

A few days later, on Nicole's twenty-fourth birthday, our family took her out to dinner. After the meal was over, I drove her and Edward back to Nicole's place. (She still lived in her grandmother Charlotte's duplex.) Edward got out of the car, but before Nicole did, I asked her if she'd stay and talk with me alone for a minute. She was immediately apprehensive.

"You want to know if I'm pregnant . . . You want me to have my tubes tied," she said suspiciously. Other guesses followed, all of them confident I was going to scold her for something. I said no to all of them and succeeded in reassuring her enough that she climbed into the front seat.

Scrunched against the car door, as far away from me as she could get, she sat there eyeing me.

"Nicole, you know I work at UCLA now," I began. Having learned how sensitive people with mental retardation are about being called retarded, I chose my words carefully. "The professors there are interested in the stories of handicapped young people—people like yourself—and I wondered if you'd let me help you write your story. We'd work on it together. Who knows? Someday it might be published."

She relaxed. The bait had been taken.

"How big would it be? Who gets the money?" she asked.

"I have no idea how many pages it would be. I also can't promise that it will be published, but if it were, you'd receive any funds that might come our way."

"I'd be so proud," she said. "It would please Grandpa so much."

I was confused. He had recently followed my mother in death. "Why?"

"He was a writer," she explained. My father had written some books. Her point was that she, too, would be an author.

Concerns began to intrude on the initial enthusiasm. "Would I have to tell . . . everything . . . ?"

"No. You'd just tell me what you want to tell me." I also promised that in any final copy she'd have the right of censorship.

She considered. Her face slowly contorted.

"You're afraid all the time I'm pregnant—or you're after me to have my tubes tied!" she cried out. "You feel I'm not capable of taking care of a baby. I **am** capable!"

No, you're not, I wanted to yell at her. But I controlled myself. "I know you're capable," I said softly.

She hardly heard me.

"You said you'd disown me if I had a child. You'd never love your own grandchild!" she wailed. I gently protested that her accusations were untrue, and tried to recapture her interest in my research proposal. No such luck. She was far too intrigued with the peculiar phenomenon of me sitting quietly instead of haranguing her. It unleashed a torrent of long-festering grievances.

"Edward said if I got pregnant, he wouldn't let me have an abortion. I know how to take care of babies. I baby-sit, even tiny ones. I took care of a really tiny one, the baby of a friend of ours. She's black, and it's black. Edward says I'm good with babies."

I gave up on my own agenda and listened sympathetically to her complaints. Finally, after forty-five minutes, she was spent. She opened the car door. One last time I asked her to consider working with me.

"I'll let you know," she said, as she began to mount the stairs leading to her apartment. "I have to think about it."

Well, so much for my great idea, I thought, as I drove home. Having witnessed all that outpouring of resentment, I was certain she'd never agree to the project.

I kept hoping, though. During the rest of the week I waited for her call. It never came.

On Saturday I called her. Fifteen times I dialed her number. The line was always busy. At 4:00 P.M. she answered.

"I had the phone off the hook so I could have some peace and quiet," she said, yawning.

It took enormous self-restraint to hide my annoyance. "I was wondering if you'd decided to work with me," I asked, as if I were commenting on the weather.

"No. I don't have time."

I dusted off the incentive of having her own story in print, but this time it held no allure.

"What are you so busy with?" I asked, stalling for

time while I thought of what strategy to try next.

"I'm starting tutoring sessions."

"Tutoring sessions?"

She was only too happy to explain. As I'd refused to release the funds in her savings account for the purchase of a moped until she had a license, she'd convinced the beneficent folk at the Department of Rehabilitation to fund her a tutor to teach her the vehicle code. Once she passed the exam, which would be administered orally, she'd have her moped license.

I was floored. Nicole's determination, if not ingenuity, was still in healthy shape. After all this time I should have been used to it, but I wasn't. I hid my amazement, however, and responded with such a disinterested "oh" that she spun a fantasy of herself on her moped tooling down the highway in helmet and boots with Edward beside her on his moped.

"Can't you fit in a few hours next week to let me record an interview with you?" I asked, when the gush of words had died.

She'd been unaware until then that I intended to record our conversations, and she saw it as one more reason not to agree to my plan. Yet the machine itself carried a certain appeal.

"Could I have the tape recorder and talk into it myself?" she asked.

"Sure," I said, grateful for any kind of encouragement. "I'll bring it right over."

The duplex where Nicole lived was in an alley by the beach. When we had moved her to the address originally, she had occupied the tiny downstairs lodgings. Six months later the more spacious upstairs apartment over the garage became vacant, and she and Edward moved up there.

Their neighborhood was a swinging one inhabited

mostly by young singles who frequented the nearby bars, ethnic cafes, and funky clothing shops. As I parked my car beside Nicole's place, rock music pulsated from a neighbor's balcony, and beach-goers streamed past in the summer sunshine: slender girls in bikinis, kids on skateboards, and bronzed hunks carrying plastic glasses of beer.

Nicole answered the door in her faded yellow housecoat. She looked as if she'd just gotten up. The apartment behind her was dark, and the television was burbling. She was so distracted by it that she barely heard my reminders of how the tape recorder worked. Any enthusiasm she'd had for dictating into a tape recorder had apparently evaporated.

"Imagine you're talking to a stranger," I told her, as I started back down the stairs, "and feel free to talk about anything you want."

The next morning, Sunday, I was surprised to receive a phone call from Nicole asking me to listen to what she'd taped. I heard a click and then, after a few seconds, a self-conscious voice.

"I moved out of my mom and dad's house when I was around nineteen or twenty-one. I began living on my own and I really liked it a lot. Then I met a guy through high school. And then we were friends for a whole year in school. And then we began dating each other and having a good time and seeing each other a lot, and I went over to his house a lot, and then he asked me to go to 'grad night,' and I couldn't go to 'grad night' because my brother was going to Greenfield—that's in Massachusetts—and I either had a choice of either going to my brother's graduation or my own graduation. And I told Edward—that's the guy I'm going with—that I was going to Greenfield to see my brother's graduation.

"Then when I got home from my trip to Greenfield with my mother and father, I was still living at home. I called Edward up because it was near my birthday, and I asked him, 'Do you want to go to Disneyland for my birthday?' and he said, 'Hey, yeah, sure,' and so we went. And then we went and picked him up at his house, his mom's house, and then we got . . . after we were all done at the very last ride at Disneyland, we went . . . that's when I was turning twenty or twenty-one . . . I don't remember exactly. . . .

"He gave me a ring, a really beautiful butterfly ring. And he asked, said to me, 'I think I love you.' And I was really, really happy, very happy. . . .

"I was still living at home, (but) I moved out like two or three months later. And then when I moved out, I moved into a place that belonged to my grandmother. And she lended it to me for a hundred and fifty, I think it was . . . I don't remember exactly. . . .

"I was working down on the beach at The Chowder Bowl. I was a short-order cook. And during that time I was still going with Edward, and he had great problems. He had very difficult problems. Number one, he didn't have a job. Number two, he didn't have any money on him. Number three, he was living at his older brother's house with his brother's girlfriend. And they were feeding him, having him have a place to live. He had a job once where his brother was working. Then he gave it up because it was too dangerous. And he was bringing home some money and some income, but still he . . . it wasn't very much. He was feeling all put down, up tight, and all riled in, and I felt sorry for him. And so I was . . . he came over to see me. I was, like, feeding him, giving him money if he needed it. I was doing everything I could possibly do. . . . "

Nicole's voice stopped. I heard Edward in the background telling her she had it all "backwards." She immediately agreed he was probably right.

"That's okay, Nicole," I reassured her. "It's the way you remembered it, and that's what's important. You did a terrific job." Hey, maybe this project is going to get underway after all, I cheered. I was so impatient to hear more, I proposed an interview for that very afternoon.

"How'd you like to come over and do your laundry? While your clothes are getting clean, you could tell me more of your story."

The trade of favors proved irresistible. Her clothes were soon churning in my machines while she sat on the floor of my bedroom, cowboy boots and bare legs folded beneath her, jabbering about the moped she was going to get and what she had cooked for dinner the night before. I let her talk until I had my tape recorder and notebook ready, and then I interrupted to begin the interview.

"Tell me, Nicole, what do you remember about your childhood?" I asked her in my best field-worker manner.

She studied me for a few seconds and then addressed me with the dignity one reserves for dealing with fools. "Why should I tell you about stuff you remember better than I do? That's dumb." She untangled her legs, stretched them out in front of her, and weighed whether the moped should be yellow or blue.

I was crushed. Again and again I tried to get her to tell me about her life. Nothing worked. All she wanted to talk about was that infuriating moped and some kind of ridiculous casserole she'd invented. After twenty minutes, I turned off the tape recorder and closed my notebook.

At least there was less tension between us. Grateful for that, I helped her fold her laundry. It was strangely pleasant—the two of us working together on a simple task. Released from the demands of my project, I relaxed and enjoyed the moment. Nicole wanted to talk about the moped and her cooking? I listened. It was a new sensation.

Gradually it dawned on me that *this* was real field work. This was what Margaret Mead did. Patiently listening and observing while sharing activities with her informants—for months, even years. This is the way you find out what a person's life is like.

All right, my daughter, I thought. This is what I'll do—if you'll let me. For two years we'll do whatever it is mothers and daughters do together, and I will piece together your perspective. You will teach me what it is like to be Nicole, a retarded woman trying to make her way in the community.

5

Mom, I know I'm retarded,
but I'm not stupid.

Nicole called me the following Tuesday evening.

"Hi," she said.

"Hi." I was right in the middle of watching a tv show I'd waited all week to see, but I turned it off.

"I just called to chat," she said.

"Okay. How are you?"

"I stayed home from work today. I was home yesterday, too. See, Sunday I threw up, and I needed a couple of days to recover."

I saw red. Nine months earlier Matt had used his influence to get her placed at Techtron in a Xeroxing job. Unlike The Chowder Bowl, Techtron paid good money and provided a magnificent array of employee benefits. Firing her would be difficult, because of company policies regarding handicapped persons, but it became immeasurably easier each day she stayed home.

I was determined to remain neutral, however. "Oh?" I said.

Nicole was quiet for a minute.

"Me and Edward and Shelley and Roger rented a boat Saturday," she revealed. Now I *knew* she was testing me. "We rented one last weekend, too."

"Did you have a nice time?" I asked, without missing a beat, even though I knew the thirty dollars should have gone toward their unpaid doctor bills and the rent which was twenty-five days overdue.

"Oh, yes," she exclaimed. As she described the motorboat ride, I tried to think of how I could get her to spend some time with me. Every few minutes I offered an invitation, but her social calendar was too full.

"How would you like a crock-pot as a late birthday present?" I asked, as a last resort. She'd often spoken of wanting one. "If you'll come to dinner tomorrow night, I'll give you one."

I could hear her weakening as she conferred with Edward. When she came back to the phone, she said they would accept.

The following evening Matt drove Nicole home from Techtron after work. Edward arrived by bicycle from their apartment, because his moped had ground to a permanent halt the week before. When dinner was over, Nicole was handed the carton containing the crock-pot. "Oooooooooooh goody," she exclaimed after she'd unwrapped it. She bent over it, her gold-rimmed glasses falling forward on her nose, as she took all the sections apart and put them back together again.

Edward, having little interest in the cookware, removed his watch and examined it.

"Why don't you give the watch to your 'father-in-law' and let him fix it?" she asked, setting the pot on the coffee table. Edward might balk at matrimony, but that didn't prevent Nicole from throwing occasional reminders his way.

Edward didn't budge.

Attention was removed from his predicament by the phone ringing. Nicole skidded into the kitchen to answer it, but Jill, who was doing the dishes, already had the receiver in her hand. "It's for me," she informed Nicole.

"Oh, phooey," chirped Nicole. After a minute, I heard ice cubes clinking into a glass. Tea, especially iced tea, was Nicole's favorite drink.

"Mom, can I go to the late movie?" asked Jill, appearing in the doorway with the phone.

"I had a feeling she was going to ask something like that," Nicole burst out. "I knew it. I knew it." Nicole's spirits were rising.

Jill hastily covered the mouthpiece of the phone with her hand and looked at me in dismay.

"Is she going to tell me to shut up?" Nicole asked me, highly amused, as she reentered the family room with her tea.

"Yeah," muttered Jill. "Mom, can I go?"

I reminded Jill that a late movie would entail being out after the curfew we'd established. Nicole listened intently. Jill finally told her caller she had to discuss the matter with her father, and she hung up.

"If you go," I cautioned Jill as she started up the stairs, "he is to come here to pick you up."

"HE! Whooooooooooooooo!" Nicole was shocked to find that her baby sister was making plans with a boy. "You're getting a hot date there, Jill," she joshed, as Jill disappeared.

Nicole looked at me and burst into laughter. "She's thinking 'Oh my God!' " she chortled, knowing full well the effect of her jibes on her sister.

"Have you met him? Does Jill like him?" she asked, as she pumped me for information about Brian, the new event in Jill's life.

"Ooooooh, this is neat," she exclaimed. "I'm so happy for her. Aren't you happy for her? You were happy when I moved out. She's going through the same difficult problems like I was, but not as bad."

"Doesn't everybody?" asked Edward softly.

"Yeah, but after she turns eighteen or twenty, she'll be wanting to move out. I was around that age, and I had trouble then. They wouldn't let me stay out to the time I wanted. . . ." She was building to a full rendition of the injustices served on her by her parents.

"I know. I know," interrupted Edward, stemming the crescendo. "I know all that."

Chastised, she sat back in her chair and folded her arms over her stocky body. "Does Brian drive a car?" she asked me.

"Yes."

"She better be careful." Nicole grinned.

"Why?" I asked.

"Oh, forget it. It's nobody's business," she decided, having second thoughts about getting into that topic with her mother.

Jill bounced down the stairs, announced she was allowed to go out with Brian, and turned on the stereo full blast to celebrate. Nicole shrieked with amusement. Edward thought Nicole was overdoing her enthusiasm. "It's *her* boyfriend, not yours," he said.

"You monkey," chirped Nicole as she bent over to nuzzle him. "I'm not going to leave you."

Jill went to get dressed for her date. I turned down the stereo, and tried to think of something neutral to discuss with Nicole and Edward.

"Do you ever go biking?" I asked.

They assured me they did. "I use mine to job hunt," Edward said.

Even though he was now unemployed, Edward had established a good work record in the past year. When he'd first moved in with Nicole, she'd taken him to the Regional Center to see if he was eligible for programs for mentally retarded persons. He tested too high. She then pushed him into completing janitorial training sponsored by the Department of Rehabilitation, but he refused to go to job interviews. Persevering, she wangled him a job working nights at The Chowder Bowl. For a year he'd washed dishes (his fingernails had become so clean he could have posed for an Ivory commercial) and waited on customers from behind the counter.

The job frightened him, however. Small in stature, he knew he was no match for the unruly customers who overflowed from the nearby pier with its bars and restaurants. When a man put his fist through the glass window that was being lowered in the process of closing the stand, Edward decided he'd had enough. He quit. He was now trying to find employment at another fast-food stand, and was making the rounds on his bicycle because his moped had died.

"Sometimes we visit Edward's sister on our bikes. She likes me a lot. She'll be my future sister-in-law," Nicole added for Edward's benefit.

Jill rejoined us, and sat down to wait for Brian.

"Do you like Nicole's cooking?" I asked Edward, continuing our conversation. He admitted he did, but he disapproved of her finishing her food and then starting in on his. When they went to have hamburgers, she always wolfed all his french fries.

"You're a little pigger," breathed Jill. Nicole whooped, and Jill winced.

"Nicole, please . . . ," begged Jill, her eye on the door where her date would be entering. (Anyone arriving by car came to the back door because our house faced a walkway to the beach instead of a street.)

Nicole was feeling so ebullient, I decided it was safe to try a more sensitive subject.

"How would you describe yourself?" I asked her.

"That's an insane question," she chortled.

"Suppose you were being hired, and the boss asked you to tell him about yourself. What would you say?"

"I got blonde hair and light colored skin like my mother's . . . and I got a hyena laugh . . . ," Nicole giggled.

"That's for sure," Edward said with a grin.

"But what if I were an employer and you had come to me about a job. What would I need to know about you?"

"I'd do good," she said, sobering a bit.

"Is there anything else I should know about you?" I pursued.

She became very quiet. "Yeah . . . I got a slow learning habit . . . I'm, I'm slightly handicapped. . . ."

As I'd expected, she avoided the label of retardation.

Brian's arrival interrupted us. Jill introduced him to everyone, and Nicole, with perfect decorum, inquired what movie they planned to see and then commented favorably on their choice.

After Jill and her date had left, Nicole carried the crock-pot to the car, and I drove her to the apartment. Edward followed on his bike.

She was quiet as we drove. Something was on her mind. Finally it came out. "Could we, uh, borrow, your camping gear for a couple of days? Andrea's new boyfriend says he'll take us up to Lake Arrowhead if you'll let us borrow it."

She had no idea how to put up the tent or start the Coleman stove and lantern. Should I say yes, and chance their being damaged? Or say no, and end the outing?

"How exciting," I said. "Of course you can use our gear. Come by Friday night on your way out of town, and we'll get it out of the garage for you."

Driving home I felt good about the evening—in spite of my uneasiness about lending her our equipment. She had certainly relaxed with me. Even Edward had been less terrified.

But more had happened than that. I felt as if I were discovering Nicole. It was as though I hadn't known her before. Everything about her was interesting.

Friday evening Nicole charged through the back gate in her cowboy boots, green argyle socks, shorts with the hem partially out, and a tank top. Close at her heels came Andrea, Edward, and what looked like two street toughs. Matt and I went out to meet them.

"This is Duke, my fiancee," announced Andrea, clinging to the shorter of the two men. Duke's T-shirt stretched across a muscled torso. He greeted us impassively, a cigarette dangling from his lips.

Andrea introduced Duke's roommate, Larry. There was a baby softness to Larry, in spite of his moustache and army fatigue cap. Shoulder-length hair framed his pock-marked face.

"Hi," he breathed in a "cool dude" manner. He had no upper teeth.

Good grief, I thought. Who are these men?

When I saw Duke's car I was even more worried. The '72 Maverick was straight out of *Tobacco Road.* The exterior had been lovingly shined, however—even the smashed-in door.

"I got a '67 Chevelle for a hundred dollars," Larry

drawled. "We just pulled the engine on it, and I'm saving to buy a new one."

As Larry detailed the plans for refurbishing his prize, Duke lugged the heavy tent out of the garage and wrestled it up to the roof of the Maverick. The roof caved in. Undismayed, Duke poked it back up again.

"Duke and me met in a bowling alley," Andrea confided to me. "I gave him my phone number." She leaned closer to me. "I can't go swimming this weekend, and Duke is mad," she added, giving me a meaningful look.

I knew then why Peggy had allowed Andrea, who still lived at home, to go off on this jaunt. Like Nicole, Andrea had resisted using birth control.

Somehow Duke got everything loaded, and everyone clambered aboard. Larry, Edward, and Nicole squeezed into the back seat where they arranged themselves around the six-packs of beer. Andrea ensconced herself on the exposed seat springs next to Duke.

"Please don't drink while you're driving," Matt begged, before they rumbled off.

"You know, it's funny," I said, after they'd turned the corner. "I'm delighted she's been accepted by those weirdos. Can you beat that? I guess parents have different standards when it comes to their retarded children."

"You can say that again. There's no way I would've let Jill go with those young men."

We spent a long weekend imagining car accidents and orgies of drugs, sex, and alcohol, yet being pleased that Nicole had found a friend as competent as Duke.

Sunday evening about five, the Maverick, now bug-splattered and dirty, rattled back up our alley. A bunch of sunburned campers trailed through the back gate.

Nicole ran into the house and immediately began

protesting that everything was in good order. Fingers and arms leaping into action, she pointed at herself, out the door, up at the ceiling—everywhere—in her effort to reassure me.

"What happened?" I asked.

"I put a hot pot on the plastic tablecloth—and it burned a hole."

Needless to say, I was relieved. "You'll just have to work around the hole the next time you use the table-cloth," I said.

She pulled me outside to inspect the dishes and utensils (they were clean and undamaged) and to see Duke. Stripped to the waist, a cigarette still dripping from his lips, he was single-handedly unloading the car.

"Duke's so good with machines he kept the car and the Coleman stove and the lantern going," she bubbled, "and he put the tent up, too."

"I got a hundred dollars saved toward my new engine," Larry started in, but he couldn't compete with Duke's and Nicole's account of their adventure. As they enlarged on it, a picture emerged of an innocuous weekend enjoyed by extremely law-abiding souls. They'd conscientiously slept in the car the first night because they arrived at the campground too late to find anyone to take their three dollar camping fee. The next day they'd obeyed the ranger when he told them not to swim because the lake "was being inspected for some kind of problem." Everyone else was in the water but not our good citizens. And when Duke drove down the mountain, it was clear he'd gone slowly.

"Cars kept hugging my rear. I kept having to pull over," he complained. "It was okay, though. I had to stop all the time anyway because Larry kept getting carsick."

I was stung by chagrin. The toughness was a thin

veneer! Duke and Larry were innocents, just youths of very limited means, delighted to have two days in the mountains for hiking, fishing, and boating. How many times had I misjudged people on the basis of first impressions? Too many. And I'd done it again.

As they took off down the alley, I called, "Come back and see us anytime. You're always welcome."

Nicole phoned a few days later. She thanked me again for the use of the camping gear and then quickly moved on to more important concerns.

"Me and Edward have made a decision," she announced. Instead of obtaining a license to ride a moped, she was going to get one for driving an automobile—Edward would, too—because they planned to buy a car.

I mentally took a sedative.

"What money do you intend to use?" I asked. She said they'd use the moped money.

Taking a big breath, I explained that the purchase price is only the beginning of a car's expenses. Money would be needed for gas, maintenance, insurance. . . .

"But it would be easier on us. We don't like to depend on other people to drive us places, and we could go on trips in a car."

"You can't AFFORD a car! You're being totally ABSURD!" That's what I wanted to scream at her but didn't.

"Even if you pass the written test, how will you learn to drive a car?" I asked.

"Driver's training. It only costs twenty dollars an hour," she said. "Is the bank open today?"

My daughter is living in a dream world. To heck with research neutrality, I decided. "Nicole," I stated, "you may not use the money in that account to buy a car."

She didn't seem surprised. "Can I still use it for a moped?"

"Yes."

She was quiet for a few seconds. "You know, me and Edward plan to get married, and sometimes . . . we've been to weddings where the bride's parents . . . uh, give, like, a car to go off in on the honeymoon. . . . but that would be asking too much, wouldn't it?" she asked, weakly.

I said nothing.

There was a long silence at her end. "Edward's having trouble finding a job," she said, greatly subdued. "He leaves his application, and they never call him. That's rude. I wish Daddy would hurry up with that job at Techtron."

"It takes time, Nicole. Edward's application is being seen by various supervisors. Your father will let you know as soon as someone agrees to interview Edward. By the way . . . how are you doing for money?"

"Just fine," she said, and changed the subject. "When're you leaving for Hawaii?"

"Tomorrow."

"I hope the plane doesn't crash."

Almost the minute Matt, Jill, and I returned from the islands, Nicole phoned.

"Me and Edward just passed our driving tests!" she shrieked. "Aren't you proud of me?"

"You did? Well, I'll be darned. . . ."

Matt and I *were* proud of her. The vehicle code contained concepts so tricky that we had seriously doubted whether she could understand it, much less memorize it. Her tutor had obviously done a good job.

"How did the Motor Vehicles people handle giving you the test when you can't read?" I asked, after Matt had congratulated both of them.

"They're very understandable. They give you a couple of chances to really try."

"How did you let them know you couldn't take a written test?"

"Oh, because I told them I'm slow in learning and that I can't read very well. When can you go to the bank?"

I started to answer, but she had more to say. The moped was merely a stopgap measure, she reminded me. Her sights were still set on a car, and she had already prevailed on the Department of Rehabilitation to provide her with driver training instruction. Lessons would begin in a few weeks.

I contemplated about the fortune to be made if I could bottle Nicole's determination and sell it.

"Why don't you and Edward come for supper again on Friday?" I suggested. "I'll have the money for you by then."

"Just a minute," she said, and she covered the phone. A muffled conversation ensued. "Edward wants to know what you're planning to serve."

I drew up a menu. He considered, and agreed to come.

Friday evening Nicole strode into the house ahead of her father, her navy deck shoes and doughnut socks pumping against the hem of her long cotton pinafore.

"Have you got the money?" she demanded.

I nodded "yes" as I completed playing the piano accompaniment for Jill's singing practice.

Reassured, Nicole turned on the tv. A beer ad came into focus on the screen showing a mountain stream swirling around boulders. She stared at it wistfully.

"Techtron is giving you a four-day weekend over Labor Day," I said, as I passed her on the way to the kitchen. "Would you like to borrow the camping gear again?"

"We're not seeing Duke and Larry anymore. Him and Andrea broke up." The news didn't surprise me. Peggy had told me that when the party returned from Lake Arrowhead, Duke had commented he was through playing Cub Scout leader.

The next day, Saturday, Matt escorted her and Edward to the moped store. Nicole scanned the row of cycles and picked out the biggest one in the shop, but when she climbed aboard, she discovered that her feet dangled. That bothered her conscientious soul.

"The D.M.V. says your feet have to touch the ground," she stated, sliding off of it.

"Well, how did you like it?" Matt asked her, when she returned from a trial spin on a model more her size.

"It runs okay," Nicole answered with an inscrutable Mona Lisa smile.

Guessing that she approved, Matt completed the business transaction.

Four days later, a series of insistent beeps on a moped horn brought Jill and me out to the alley. There sat a smug Nicole astride her new machine. Jill's and my attention was distracted from the shiny green moped by Nicole's colorful garb—pink and red striped socks pulled up to mid-calf, the usual deck shoes, a full skirt of dainty flowers showing below a huge fluorescent orange windbreaker, and a helmet that nearly covered her face. But we examined all the finer points of the moped and congratulated Nicole on her excellent choice.

Before she rode off down the alley with horn beeping and turn signals flashing, I glanced at the odometer.

In four days she'd driven 161 miles.

Early in September Techtron arranged two interviews for Edward. They were both on the same day. At 5:40 P.M. on the day before they were to occur, the phone rang.

"I went to get a haircut and I've got a flat tire," Edward burst out. "Bill's got the moped in his car, and we have to take it to the shop right away because it closes in twenty minutes! I have to ride it to Techtron tomorrow! Has Nicole gotten there yet?"

"Edward, I'm confused. . . ."

"Nicole has to come home right away!" Edward persisted.

I heard the car door slam in our garage. "Hang on, Edward. She's here. You can talk directly to her."

She grabbed the phone and signaled for me to be quiet so she could hear him. As she talked with him, her excitement drew Jill and Matt to the scene. Hovering, they badgered her with questions until they learned that Edward needed Nicole to come home because she had the money to pay for the tire repair. Matt and Jill began offering advice. Especially Jill.

Nicole's voice rose as she tried to cope with both Edward's frantic pleas and the conflicting directives from her family. The pressure was too much. Arms rigidly at her sides, face flushed, lips clamped tight, she turned to Jill and released a muffled, throat rattling squeal.

"I can't stand it!" she screamed. Chastened, we all backed away.

Nicole turned to the phone and instructed Edward to go to the moped shop without her and get the man started on the tire repair. Bill and he could then come to our house to pick her up, and they would all return to the shop together to pay for the work.

She hung up and retreated to the kitchen for some badly needed tea.

Matt went upstairs. Jill resumed laying out pattern pieces over her sewing material on the floor. I didn't move. Nicole's solution was better than any her family had offered. And she'd arrived at it under pressure.

I followed her into the kitchen and began to praise her.

"Mom," she interrupted, "I know I'm retarded, but I'm not stupid."

I started to laugh, but it seemed the wrong thing to do, so I choked it off.

"I don't understand this cutting layout," Jill called. Nicole nearly knocked me down as she flew out of the kitchen. "I'm sorry I got mad at you," she said to her sister, clinging to Jill's hand and patting it.

"It's okay," Jill said. "I'm sorry I got so excited."

Suddenly Nicole stopped and studied Jill. "She's changed," Nicole said to me. "I don't know what it is, but she's changed." Her voice was suffused with admiration.

Jill laughed with the graciousness of a queen as she glanced at herself in a mirror behind Nicole's head. Nicole had become conscious of what we all had been observing over the summer: Jill was turning from a gangly child into a young woman. The bikini she was wearing displayed the transformation.

Self-conscious over being the focus of so much attention, Jill asked me about her sewing problem. As she and I discussed it, Nicole sat down on the two steps leading into the family room to watch her.

"I wish I was thin like that," she said, her eyebrows peaking in an inverted "V." "I want to be able to wear a cute little bathing suit like she's wearing." She chewed on her finger, and her eyes began to glisten. "Edward wants me to lose weight. He wants me to join Watch Weighters."

I thought a second. "Weight Watchers?"

"Yeah."

I bent over and kissed her forehead. "That might be a good idea," I said.

Matt, who had come back downstairs, tried to cheer her up. "You could begin your diet by cutting out the organic food . . . ," he commented, as he tied the shoelaces on his Nikes.

Nicole looked at him quizzically.

" . . . like fingernails."

Nicole jerked her finger out of her mouth, erupted into her "hyena" guffaw, and banged both feet on the stairstep below. We all joined her in laughter, welcoming the opportunity to end an awkward moment.

Matt left for his evening jog. I helped Jill arrange her pattern pieces, and returned to the kitchen. Nicole followed. While I unloaded the dishwasher, she informed me that she wished she had a dishwasher. As I expected, the dishwasher was merely the first in her list for the evening. She wanted a sewing table like mine, a new refrigerator, a new stove, our microwave oven—should I decide I didn't want it, a "big, fancy" sofa, and two end tables. While she was at it, she informed me that Edward's teeth should be refurbished.

"His teeth are very bad," she fretted. "I tell him to brush them, but he always forgets. He needs to go to the dentist." Edward was proving intransigent on this score. He couldn't remember ever having been to a dentist, and he saw little point in going now.

Her face clouded as she thought about Edward. "He's unpatient with me," she said, darkly.

I looked at her.

"I don't want to talk about it," she said..

What was going on between them? I worried.

A car horn sounded, and Nicole ran out to the alley. I followed and said hello to Bill. I hadn't seen him since the car pools for the Go-Getters. It surprised me to realize that he was a man now, complete with five o'clock shadow.

"Edward's at the shop," he said. Nicole slipped into the front seat, and off they went.

Edward made it to both interviews, and we waited anxiously to hear whether a job offer would be extended.

A week later Matt came home with a long face. "He didn't make it. Neither supervisor wanted him."

"Oh, Matt, how awful."

Matt sat down in an armchair, paused to gather his courage, and dialed Nicole's number. Edward answered. Matt told him the news as gently as he could.

Edward said nothing.

Two nights later, at 11 P.M., Nicole called.

"Can I have David's phone number?" she asked in a strained voice.

"Certainly," I answered. I stated it very slowly so she could write it down.

About fifteen minutes later David called. Nicole had called him, crying. She and Edward were out of money. Edward had lost both jobs at Techtron. She might not have a position herself soon because she'd been so worried that she had stayed home for the past three days.

I dialed her number immediately. "May I speak with Nicole?" I asked, when Edward answered the phone. I heard him tenderly urging her not to cry as he handed it to her.

"I didn't want to involve you," she said. Her voice shuddered with barely controlled sobs. "I'm trying to solve my problems without bothering anyone."

"I know, honey."

"You're so lucky to have a super husband. He has lots of money. You have a lovely home and three cars, a refrigerator, a microwave. . . ."

"Most people don't live the way we do," I protested. "Your father and I scraped for years and years."

"But the way I'm going, I'm never going to be able to have those things. I try to do a good job at work, but I'll never be able to make that kind of money." Her voice was charged with suffering.

This was the daughter I thought was living in a dream world?

"I need to bring home a lot higher amount, like Dad does. He's bringing home near 300 something, isn't he? Bill does, too. He can afford a car, gas, insurance, nice clothes. . . ."

"Bill still lives with his parents," I reminded her. "He doesn't have the expenses you do."

She blew her nose and left the phone to get more Kleenex.

As I waited for her to return, I marveled at the way she was describing her predicament. Although her distress was clearly caused by Edward's joblessness, she wasn't angry with him, didn't blame him, didn't even threaten him with eviction. Instead, she said her own income was inadequate.

When she returned to the phone, I asked whether Edward had any other job possibilities besides Techtron.

"I've been trying to get him to go back to The Chowder Bowl, but he won't because of the fights and the rowdy people."

"Well, is he continuing to try places like McDonalds and Jack-in-the-Box?"

"All he ever hears is 'We'll call you.' "

It was 12:30 A.M., and I was exhausted. She wanted to continue, but I reminded her we both had to go to work in the morning.

"I love you," I said in closing. Hearing my voice, I was incredulous. Did I say that? The declaration came out as the most natural thing in the world.

"I love you, too, Mom," she answered.

I hung up determined to get Edward a job—despite Nicole's view of the situation. A few days later, I spoke with his former supervisor at The Chowder Bowl who reassured me that although Edward was often sick and his slowness sometimes irritated the customers, he was an excellent employee. Armed with that information, I approached the manager of Joey's, where Edward had recently left an application.

"He's very shy," I explained. "But he's worked at The Chowder Bowl for two years and has a good record."

"Someone else must have interviewed him," the manager said, after she looked up his application. "They made no notation why he wasn't hired. Would you like me to interview him myself?"

I assured her I would be grateful if she would. After she set a time for the interview, I ran across the street to a phone booth.

"Huh," Nicole grunted, when she answered after many rings. She hadn't gone to work again, I noted with dismay.

"Hi," I greeted her. "Let me speak to Edward."

"He's asleep," she mumbled.

"Well, wake him up."

He took the phone, and I told him the news. "Be there at four o'clock sharp," I coached, "and look eager."

At supper that night Nicole called. "Daddy? Edward wants to talk to you."

"It looks like I may have a job," Edward exclaimed to Matt. "I go in to Joey's tomorrow for orientation and uniform measurement."

Matt passed the news to the rest of us, and everyone cheered.

Matt handed the phone to me, and Edward thanked me for interceding on his behalf. His voice was more confident than I'd ever heard it. It was also a number of decibels louder.

Nicole came on the phone. "I feel so much better," she said. She'd already planned how they would spend the double income. "We're going to get both television sets 'prepaired' "—the one they'd retrieved from a neighbor's trash, as well as "the other one"—"and we're going to buy a new sofa, two end tables, two lamps, a coffee table. . . ."

The following week I had another opportunity to show off the photographs of my children. I still didn't have a picture of Nicole, however.

"You have just the two children?" the student asked as we waited for our seminar to begin.

"No. I have an older daughter. She's . . . ." I stopped. Suddenly I couldn't say "retarded." I realized that using that label was a way of dismissing her. It was like saying "Now that I've told you that, you know everything about her."

But the label didn't fit Nicole. Maybe it didn't fit *other* retarded people either. I had a tremendous urge to tell the student about the real Nicole—

—the stocky figure careening down the alley on

her moped with turn signals flashing and horn beeping, her flowered skirt billowing over brightly striped socks and cowboy boots.

—the flirtatious girl snuggling up to her boyfriend with teasing eyes to reassure him she has no intention of leaving him.

—the wistful woman, eyes filling with tears, who suddenly has noticed the slim, blossoming body of her fifteen-year-old sister.

—the daughter, rigid and flushed, who finds she must scream at her family in order to assert her right to handle her own affairs.

—the giddy creature who drums her feet in delight over her father's wisecrack.

I wanted to tell this girl—anyone—that Nicole was all of this and so much more. But the class discussion was beginning.

6

Can't do nuthin'
on the amount I make.

Edward joined the ranks of the employed in October. Back in June, when I'd taken Nicole on as my informant, I'd had to pursue her. No longer. She was now calling every day. Sometimes she had news. Usually she just wanted contact.

"Hello?"

"Heating and plumbing!" She followed her greeting with muffled squeaks and then peals of laughter. "Did I fool you? Did you think it was a plumbing store?"

"I rather guessed it was you, Nicole."

"Heating and plumbing! Heating and plumbing!" she chortled over and over, enjoying her joke.

"Edward looks so nice in his uniform," she said, at long last. "He works the cash register and everything."

She reviewed a number of topics during these calls, many of them quite repetitively. There was one, though, that she always managed to avoid—their financial situation. She kept a high wall around that topic.

During an unexpected visit to our house one Saturday afternoon, however, the wall cracked.

"I don't like telling you our business," she began, when she and Edward walked in our door that day. "I feel it's not right nor nothin'. . . . "

I steeled myself. *She wants something from me.*

"Would you like a sandwich?" I asked. I was making one for myself.

She shook her head. "I feel embarrassed coming to you." Similar introductory remarks continued until she'd mustered enough nerve to get to the point of her visit. By that time, if she'd had a tail, she would have been wagging it.

"Me and Edward want to move," she said, bringing her face so close to mine she bumped my forehead, "and we need you to give us the deposit money."

Oh, great. First it was a car. Now it's money for a new apartment.

"Why do you want to move?" I asked, putting down the knife. I couldn't see the tomato I was slicing because her face was in the way.

She straightened up. Her arms and fingers flying, she described the plaster that was falling off the ceiling, the jammed bathroom window, the kitchen drawer handle that fell off. . . .

"It's difficult for Charlotte to afford repairs," I reminded her, "when the rent you pay is only half what she'd charge any other tenant."

"Yes, I know," she said, deftly detouring around my explanation, "but, see, we visited these friends last night. They live in a lots nicer place, and they pay only $300. And their apartment lady showed us this empty apartment, and it's got carpeting and a built-in stove, and. . . . "

"Nicole, you can't find the $265 to pay for your present apartment. How can you afford $300 for this other one?"

"Penny and Francisco can afford it, and they're both on SSI," she countered, trailing closely behind me as I carried my sandwich to the family room table. I'd never heard of these people before, but Nicole frequently spoke of friends unknown to me.

"Well, perhaps you can afford it," I said, foxily. "Before I can figure that out, though, you'll have to tell me how much money you both make."

"Edward—tell my mom," she said, without hesitation.

He had sat down to watch tv when he entered the house, but he turned it off and sidled over to the table. "I brought home $90 last week," he began. "Sometimes Nicole's check is $108, sometimes $80 . . . "

"It goes up and down," Nicole snorted. "I don't know why."

Was she truly unaware of the connection between her paycheck amount and her malingering? I couldn't tell.

I did a little math on my napkin. "Suppose we say Nicole's check is $100 a week, and yours is $90. That's about $760 a month. So . . . you have $160 more to work with than Penny and Francisco, because two people on SSI only get $600."

"We *can* live there then, can't we?" Nicole asserted.

"Perhaps." I took a bite of my sandwich. "Do you have any bills—any money you owe—other than your rent?"

Nicole and Edward exchanged glances.

"Go ahead and tell her," Nicole shrugged.

"Yeah, at the clinic," Edward said.

"How much do you owe there?"

Edward frowned as he tried to remember. "The last

statement said $190, I think."

I began to understand why she was so reluctant to talk about their money.

"If you married me, you'd be covered by my medical insurance," Nicole sniped.

"I don't understand how to fill out the forms! And I never know what's been paid and what hasn't!" he retorted and turned to me. "Some of that $190 is Nicole's."

That was entirely possible. Her insurance had a $200 deductible.

"Do you have any other bills?" I asked.

Edward considered. "Well, the phone bill is always big. Like last month it was sixty dollars and something."

Good grief! Were they calling Hawaii?

He began fishing in Nicole's purse for the checkbook. She grabbed his hand, and then changed her mind. "Oh, go ahead," she said. "Stupid, stupid checkbook. They keep bouncing my checks, the bank does. And everytime they make me pay four dollars." Just thinking about it made her so angry, she shoved back her chair and stamped into the kitchen to make some tea.

Edward found the checkbook and opened it. "Here it is—$63.20."

"Why was it so high?"

"Nicole called Hawaii and Wisconsin. She has friends there."

He handed me the checkbook. It was full of entries not only to supermarkets but also to restaurants, movie houses, and stereo record shops. They were living The Good Life.

"Can we afford the apartment?" Nicole asked, returning with her tea.

"Sure, if you manage your money better."

Nicole hooted. "Grandma Charlotte always talks like that. She tells us we don't know how to handle our money. How else can people enjoy themselves— without staying home and worrying about the stupid rent and blah, blah, blah, blah, blah?"

"Perhaps you'd like your father or me to help. For a while you could bring us twenty-five or fifty dollars a week and we could pay your bills for you—until you get caught up. We could also show Edward how to keep track of your medical insurance."

"No way," declared Nicole, shaking her head emphatically. "That's not making it on your own."

I returned to my sandwich. "Would you like an orange?" I asked, indicating a bowl of oranges on the table. "They're from your father's ranch."

Neither of them responded. "Are you going to give us the money for the deposit?" Nicole asked, after a bit.

"No. It wouldn't make sense to help you move to a more expensive apartment when you can't manage to pay your present rent."

Edward shifted uneasily in his seat. Nicole seized her spoon and began agitatedly turning it over and over on the table top.

"We can't live on what we bring in!" she exploded. "It's stupid. I need to bring in the amount Daddy makes."

"Let's go, Nicole," Edward said softly.

"Can't do nuthin' on the amount I make," she groused. "I hate telling people about my problems."

"Come on, Nicole . . . "

Edward kept nudging her until she got up and moved toward the door. When she reached it, she turned back to me.

"Oh, forget it," she said, and they were gone.

She doesn't understand money any better than she did before leaving home, I thought. I cursed our affluence. Surely frugality would have come easier if Matt and I were poor. But still, she *had* to learn to live within her income. I was as convinced of that as I'd ever been.

I was less convinced about other notions I'd been clinging to since she left home. One was her job. I'd been so positive that she was lucky to be at Techtron. Lately, as I listened to her complaints, I'd begun to wonder.

One night she expressed herself more vehemently than usual.

She'd stopped by on her way home from work. As she entered the house, my first thought was about her appearance. Her blouse was held together by a large safety pin from which dangled a button. Her legs were bare beneath her culottes, and the pom-poms on her socks were slipping down into her worn-out oxfords. I wondered how much the way she looked affected how her fellow employees felt about her.

"Hi. What's up?" I asked while I continued to peel potatoes.

She unbuckled her helmet. Her eyes were narrowed.

"It's your job," I guessed. "How's it going?"

"It's okay. Besides for one person . . . who's an ASS HOLE," she hissed.

I winced. "Who? Your supervisor?"

"No. I don't want to talk about it." She sprawled across the kitchen counter. "I just want to sit and watch tv and forget about the world. I'm sick of turning pages and pages and pages. I don't think I'm ever going to get moved into something different."

She was probably right. Since she'd been at Techtron she'd been locked into the same task, "turning pages," hour after hour, day after day, standing by her hot reproduction machine with the flashing light and nerve-wracking noise, while her fellow employees were given more varied tasks.

"It's up to you whether to quit or not," I said.

"I don't want to quit," Nicole protested. "I need the money. It's just that I want to do different things. 'Proreduction' is so boring!" She jerked her sleeve up and began digging at her arm. From wrist to elbow it was covered with ugly sores.

"This person you say is mean—is there anyone in your office you like?" I asked, as I grieved over her arm.

"Yes. There's one lady who's nice to me. Her name is Barbara." She shook her head. "No. That's not her name. . . . " Her forehead pinched in concentration. "I can't remember it."

Her inability to name even one friend said worlds about her social life at Techtron.

"If Edward were making enough money, I'd just stay home and be a housewife," she asserted. "Penny does that. I could, too."

The phone rang. It was Edward.

"I gotta go," she said, putting her helmet back on and heading out the door. "Edward's hungry."

When Matt came home from work a few minutes later, he listened gravely as I told him about Nicole's bitterness.

"You know," he said, "it isn't only the job itself. She has long days. She gets up at 6:00 A.M., rides her moped through every kind of weather on a trip to the plant that may take twenty minutes, works from 8:00 until 5:00 with an hour off for lunch, rides back home, and then has to fix supper. That's a grueling schedule for anyone."

I slowly wiped my hands on a dish towel.

"Matt . . . ?"

"Yes?"

"Did we do the wrong thing in finding her a job at Techtron?"

He squinted his eyes in thought as he looked out the window. "No. Her days may be hard, but so are yours and mine. It isn't right for anybody to stay home and watch tv if they're capable of working."

He went upstairs to change clothes. I wondered if Nicole would be better off on SSI—if she could still get it.

I was also beginning to be less sure that she should live in our beach community. My concern had been one of safety. The towns where people in her income bracket lived had a higher crime rate.

But one day I took her to a recycling center in Fremont, a low income community, and I came home with something new to consider.

Before we left Soleado Beach, we had stopped in a service station for gas. Nicole stood out among the stylish patrons. With her hooded eyes, pudgy legs, bare feet, and old gym suit held together by a safety pin at the shoulder, she was an oddity, and people glanced at her curiously.

The response was quite different at the recycling center. There, no one paid any attention to her. Among people whose skin colors and facial features ranged from A to Z and whose clothing styles were dictated more by availability than fashion, she blended in. Even the difficulty she had in writing her name was accepted as ordinary.

Should she be living in Fremont? I asked myself. True, there were bars on a few shop windows and graffiti on some walls, but Duke and Larry lived there. Good people like them lived everywhere.

Not long after that, I was forced to reexamine another of my cherished beliefs. I'd been so confident that Nicole had to learn to manage her time. After all, it was the key to being punctual.

At first I blamed her friends. Most of them were on SSI, or they worked only part-time, and as they had no early morning deadline to meet, they felt free to drop by evenings and visit until all hours. Nicole got nothing constructive done while they were there, and the next day she was invariably late for work.

I resented the seductive influence of these friends until I saw her with them for the first time.

The occasion was Thanksgiving. Shelley was at Nicole's apartment when I dropped by in the morning. A tall young woman with large eyes and an apologetic manner, Shelley was an only child who lived with her widowed father. He was concerned about her, but he had needs of his own. Shelley, as a result, spent much of her time at Nicole's apartment.

Edward enjoyed having her around. When Nicole was busy taking charge of everything, as she invariably did, he and Shelley had fun together. That morning they were playing with Edward's new walkie-talkies.

Nicole ran out of the kitchen and pulled me in to see what she had done. With squeals of excitement and tears of pride, she showed me a turkey browning in the oven and two freshly baked mincemeat pies whose top crusts resembled the cloud swirls on Venus. The aroma was so heavenly my knees went weak.

"Nicole," I said, "I'm impressed. I am truly impressed."

Unable to choose between crying and laughing, she twisted her hands in her apron and did a little of both.

"Tell your mom how late you and Shelley were up last night," Edward called to her.

Nicole giggled and wiped a tear away.

"They were cooking until 3:00 A.M.!" Edward shouted.

"Shelley read me the recipes," Nicole said.

Her friend appeared in the doorway, unsure whether to enter.

"Aren't you lucky to have such a good friend who will stay up late and read you recipes?" I said to Nicole.

Shelley's Spaniel eyes glowed with pleasure.

"Were the pies made from scratch?" I asked Shelley.

"No," said Nicole, answering for her. "The bottom crust was frozen, and the top one was a package. The mincemeat came from that jar."

Nicole glanced at the clock. (She could tell time easily now.) "Wow. I gotta get to work." She plunged her hands into the dishwater. "I gotta do these and make the bed and. . . . "

"Couldn't Shelley and Edward help?"

"Oh, no. It's my job. Men aren't supposed to do housework, and Shelley is our guest."

Shelley smiled at me and shrugged her shoulders.

"Are you still coming over after dinner at Grandma Charlotte's?"

"Absolutely," I said, heading out the door into the chilly ocean air.

When Matt and I knocked on her door that afternoon, we were met by a mob of laughing young people who swept us into the living room. Nicole, still in the blue and white striped gym suit she'd had on that morning, led the pack. Whooping uncontrollably, she dragged me to the buffet arranged on top of her desk and pointed out the turkey carcass and the nearly empty bowls of stuffing, mashed potatoes, and gravy. Suddenly she vanished. I looked through the crowd but she was gone.

"She just threw up again," Edward said, his eyes indicating the kitchen, as he rushed past me on his way to the bathroom.

I found a wan Nicole in the kitchen. "I guess I got too excited," she said.

"What a shame to lose Thanksgiving dinner," I commiserated, as Edward cleaned up the mess with the bathroom sponge.

"Hey, Nicole, c-c-c-come finish s-s-s-serving the pie," called a young man with a stutter. It was Roger.

Considerably sobered, Nicole reentered the living room, cut his piece, and then cut pieces for everyone else. Matt and I settled ourselves on the couch to eat ours.

Looking up between bites, I suddenly recognized Mary Brichant, Edward's mother, sitting on the beanbag chair in the corner. The last time we had seen each other was when I had picked Edward up from her apartment to take him to Disneyland.

We got up and hugged in greeting. "Forgive me for not seeing you," I exclaimed.

"I didn't want to intrude," she said.

With demure excitement she told me about her new job keeping house for an elderly woman, a position she was finding more pleasant than the previous one cooking in a convalescent home. As I listened to her talk, I remembered Edward's telling me about the years of abuse she had endured from his alcoholic father, and how she had finally left him to raise their four children alone. It was hard to believe she had had that strength, her manner was so sweet and reticent. We chatted about our children's successful Thanksgiving party, and the cold weather, and then returned to our respective places to finish our pie.

As I ate, I tried to figure out who everyone else was. I knew Roger. Always impeccably clothed and groomed, today he'd added a bow tie to set off his plaid sports coat and slacks. Bill I scarcely recognized. He'd been seriously ill since I last saw him, and haunted eyes stared out of his cadaverous face.

The others were strangers. An overweight couple (were they Penny and Francisco?). A bald man with steel-rimmed glasses. A diminutive woman who nodded agreeably to everything the bald man said. A fellow with wrinkled clothes and uncombed hair whose gaze, I noticed when he glanced my way, wasn't true.

Were these the nocturnal visitors? I wished I could ask.

Whoever they were, Nicole was thoroughly enjoying playing hostess to them. I began to have second thoughts about condemning the time she spent with friends, even if they kept her up until 1:00 A.M. on week nights.

Over the next week I told myself that time management involved a lot more than merely controlling the hours spent with friends. Nicole's attention drifted, and she dawdled, whether friends were present or not.

She was simply going to have to become more efficient. Or so I thought—until she and I went Christmas shopping.

"I need help choosing gifts," she'd said when she called the day before we went. "Can you take me tomorrow?"

"All right. What time?" I would go, but only if I could set a limit on how long we'd spend at the mall.

"Two o'clock."

"No—10:30. And I have to be home by 1:30. I can't take all day."

I arrived at her apartment at 11:00 to give her plenty of time. Edward let me in. I picked my way through the debris of pizza crusts and empty soda pop cans on the living room floor, and poked my head into the kitchen.

Nicole was dumping a pan of water into the sink. "I get so tired of melting the ice off this dumb, stupid thing," she groused. "Someday I'm going to get a disfreezable one."

Twenty minutes later she turned the refrigerator back on and trailed into the bedroom. I followed. The furniture set she'd purchased so defiantly two summers ago could scarcely be seen in the disarray.

At the end of the dresser was a vine. It emerged, naked, from dry dirt, leaned over the edge of its pot and hung down the dresser onto the floor. At its tip was a single leaf.

"How often do you water your plants, Nicole?" I asked. "This one looks like it could stand a little more."

"They need to be dry," she said, as she pulled her purse out from under the bed. "It makes them strong."

When we finally got into my car, I tried to make up for the time we had lost.

"I'm not going to drive this fast when I get *my* license," Nicole said, gripping the armrest on the door.

As soon as we arrived at the shopping mall, I whipped out my notebook and pen. "Okay, now. Let's make a list. Who do you have to get presents for?"

She named the people, one by one, and I wrote them down. That done, I dived into the department store next to us to buy some socks for her to give Jill.

"Oooooooh, Mom . . . " she gasped, as soon as we were inside. "Look at the wedding rings! Me and Edward are going to get ones like these." She bent over the jewelry case to gaze at them.

Hiding my impatience, I inspected the rings and then headed again for the escalator. Arriving there, I looked back. She was gone again.

"Nicole?"

"Over here, Mom," she yelled. I found her in a display of stereo equipment. "That's the one Edward wants to buy," she sighed as she inspected a state-of-the-art component in chrome and walnut.

"Nicole, socks are upstairs," I said, as I herded her toward the escalator. We rode up to the third floor, and stepped off.

"Oooooooh, aren't these pretty?" she cooed, as she ran to a stack of soft blankets and hugged a pink one. "I could get this for Edward's Aunt Gertrude."

"Nicole. . . . "

"See, it goes with these sheets. I'd like cute little matching stuff like that for my bed."

"Nicole. . . . "

"Oooooooh, look." A display of silver had sent its siren call, and she went scurrying over to see it.

I looked at my watch. It was now 12:30. Why didn't she understand that shopping must be tackled single-mindedly and dispatched as quickly as possible? Why was she wasting time looking at all these frivolous things?

Then I understood. Shopping was what *I* was doing. She had a different agenda. All the things she'd ever wished for were within touching distance for a few hours. That was all that mattered. The mall was Disneyland without the rides.

I put the shopping list away and fell in beside her. Together we marveled at the glistening coffee pots and tea services. We smelled fragrant soaps in floral wrappers, stroked luxurious mink coats, admired the lush colors and soft texture of silk dresses, dabbed on perfume from fragile bottles, cuddled Siberian husky puppies, and played video games.

It was strangely pleasant drifting in a different time warp, one where the words "hurry" and "do" hadn't been invented yet.

At one point, we pulled ourselves together enough to buy Nicole a dress, but the task proved so arduous that we needed two leisurely sipped cups of tea to recover.

Revived, we strolled along again, arm in arm, humming "Rudolph, the Red Nosed Reindeer" to the organ music filling the air. A display window containing baby clothing lured Nicole, and we floated into the shop. I'd given up looking at my watch hours ago.

"Oooooooh, little girl clothes," she said, taking down a tiny pink dress with ruffles at the hem. "I want dresses like this for my little girl."

She turned the dress on its hanger and looked at it wistfully. Slowly she replaced it and then went down the row of infant outfits, examining each one. "They're so adorable. I'd like to buy one for Annie Lee's new baby." Annie Lee was one of her cousins.

I watched her with a pang. All the cousins that she'd grown up with were now having babies. *How difficult it must be for you being childless, seeing them with their infants. And to think I scolded you about not using birth control. . . .*

Suddenly Nicole threw her arms around me and kissed me. "I love shopping with you, Momma," she exclaimed. I was so startled, I dropped the quilt I'd picked up, and held her close.

How long had it been since she'd hugged me? I couldn't remember. If this was the reward for my field work, it was enough. Let the other shoppers stare.

"I'm so glad we had the day alone together," she said, giving me another kiss.

After I dropped her off at her apartment, I drove home, glowing.

But I was also a bit shaken. The mall experience had made me acutely aware of how goal-oriented Matt and I were. Every day, seventeen hours a day, we planned ahead and raced to accomplish our objectives. That was fine for us, but did Nicole have to live that way?

It seemed as if I was becoming shaky about everything regarding Nicole.

The mother is charming just as much as Nicole

In the next few weeks, I was too busy surviving Christmas to have time for further reflection. Nicole was preoccupied, too. She found time to keep up with her television viewing, however. One night just before Christmas, she called because she was perplexed about one of the shows.

"Are you watching 'Joseph and Mary'?" she asked David, who had answered the phone.

"Yes," he said.

"Can I ask you a question? Why is Mary wearing that veil?"

"Because she's a virgin," he said, trying to watch the show.

"Oh." She considered a moment, and then hung up.

About ten minutes later she called back. I answered this time.

"Was Mary a virgin?"

"Yes," I said.

"Does that mean Joseph wasn't Jesus's father? God was?"

"That's what the Bible says."

I could fairly hear the cogs whirring in her brain.

"Would you go get me the Bible and read me the part that explains how that happened?"

"I wish I could, Nicole, but no details were supplied."

For the next five minutes she railed against the flagrancy of this gap in historical documentation. Finally, however, she added God's insemination of Mary to her long list of life's unsolved mysteries.

That done, she began whispering. "The case of moped oil is all wrapped and under our tree. Edward keeps lifting it. He can't figure it out."

Her restraint concerning our present to Edward amazed us. For two months she and Shelley both had known we were giving him a moped. They'd helped Matt pick it out, and even bought accessories and moped oil. Yet they'd never once leaked the secret to Edward.

Nicole even managed to control her excitement on Christmas morning. When she and Edward arrived at our house, her eyes darted around the family room until they found the moped covered with an old blanket. It was in a far corner, almost hidden under the piano. She seated Edward with his back to it.

After we turned the Christmas carols down and quieted Bartok, our sheltie, we all turned to Edward.

"Why don't you go look over by the piano, Edward?" I suggested.

He dutifully rose, walked over there, and looked at us.

"Lift the blanket," Matt said.

He pulled it half off and stopped. His face was a blank.

"It's for you, Edward," Jill said.

"You gotta be kidding," he breathed, and retreated to his chair. Nicole, at last freed to express her excitement, squealed and bounced up and down in her chair.

"Come on back," Matt ordered. "I have to take your picture." Edward returned, stood somberly while flashbulbs popped, and hustled again to the chair.

Later, when the present unwrapping hullabaloo and breakfast were over, he approached the shiny black machine with black leatherette saddlebags and wheeled it out the door. In the alley where the garage obstructed our view of him, he examined his prize in private.

Shortly after that, he and Nicole rode home. Matt and I assumed we wouldn't see them again that day, because they'd been invited to Mary Brichant's for dinner. But at eight o'clock that night, Nicole burst in the door.

"Mom! Dad!" she shrieked.

Convinced something terrible had happened, Matt and I tore down the stairs.

She and Edward stood there, beaming like they'd just won first prize in a fashion show. Nicole had on the dress I'd bought her in the mall, and Edward sported a navy blue three-piece suit replete with shirt, tie, and patent leather shoes.

"How handsome you are," I exclaimed. "Are you on your way to Edward's mom's?"

"No. Everything got mixed up. It's very complicated. We're not going anywhere. We just wanted to show you our new clothes."

David came bounding down the stairs with Jill right behind him. Both were in party attire. "Hey, you guys look pretty nifty," David commented to Nicole and Edward, as he looked in the mirror and adjusted his bow tie.

"Where'd you get the cool new suit?" Jill asked.

"At Pennimart. It cost twenty dollars," Edward said, grinning. Nicole laughed with pride over their successful bargain hunting.

"Dad, I took your keys," David said, as he headed for the door. "I can't find mine. Okay if I use your car?"

"I suppose so. Make sure it has gas in it."

Nicole intercepted her brother at the door. Wrapping him in a hug, she laid her head on his chest.

"Can Edward and me go?" she asked coyly, blinking her eyes up at him.

He glanced at me. "No, Nicole, I'm sorry." He gently disentangled her arms. Nicole watched him through the glass-paned door as he crossed the patio and strode out the gate.

"Is my string of pearls fastened okay, Mom?" Jill asked. She lifted her hair off the back of her neck so I could inspect the clasp.

"It's just fine. David is taking you to Laurie's?"

She nodded.

"Who's bringing you home?"

"Brian."

"Remember your curfew," Matt called, as she scurried after her brother.

Nicole didn't bother to ask Jill if she and Edward could be included in *her* plans. The answer, she already knew, would be no. She stood looking out the door until Jill closed the gate behind her.

The house was suddenly quiet.

"Where are you and Dad going?" she asked, turning and noticing that we were dressed up.

"A party. I wish we could take you," I added, "but it wouldn't be the thing to do. We thought you'd be busy with Edward's family tonight."

"No problem," she said, too quickly. "Edward and me will have a nice evening by ourselves."

"You can stay here and watch tv. . . . "

She looked at Edward but he shook his head.

"No, we'll enjoy the ride home on our mopeds," she said. "Then we'll light candles and have some supper."

The hurt was well hidden. She made it sound as if they'd had that plan all along.

"Thanks for the moped," Edward said shyly, as he rose and joined her at the door.

Matt and I watched them go. They'd accepted the rejection so quietly. No complaints. No indication at all of their feelings.

But then, that was typical. Nicole rarely talked about being excluded. The only time I could recall she had was during a phone call a week or so before Christmas.

"Guess where we went today! 'Movie World'!" she'd exclaimed to me on that occasion.

"'Movie World'?"

"Yeah, and we saw where Steve Austin and Jamie Sommers got their operation. But they didn't really get one." In a jumble of words she tried to explain the magic that "The Six Million Dollar Man" technicians could perform to fool the viewer. I finally concluded they'd visited Universal Studios.

"We had such a good time I'd like to go back with Jill and her sweetie, Brian," Nicole exulted. She paused. "If they wouldn't be offended by us," she quietly added.

I hung up and thought about those words, "if they wouldn't be offended by us." What would it be like to know that all the "normal" people in the world, even brothers and sisters, merely tolerated you? To know that they would never permit the close sharing of reciprocated friendship?

One night in January, the myriad challenges to my accustomed way of thinking about Nicole suddenly fit together. At first I thought I'd uncovered her perspective. Then I realized I had merely gained insight into my own.

She had called that night, requesting a favor. "I hate to ask this, but could you drive me to Dottie's?"

Dottie, I had learned since Thanksgiving, was the young woman who had given all her attention to Todd, the bald man, at Nicole's dinner. Todd and Dottie were getting married, and tonight was her wedding shower.

"Roger was supposed to pick me up, but I guess he forgot," Nicole said. Something was wrong. Her voice was shaking.

"We'll be right there," I assured her.

In a few minutes Matt and I were at her apartment. Matt honked the horn, and she came down the stairs.

She looked very much the modish young office worker with her funky sandals, hosiery, wrap-skirt, jersey blouse, and bulky sweater. Her hair was freshly combed and slicked back into a neat little bun.

I let her into the back seat, and she sat with her eyes down.

"The present is in the paper bag. I didn't have time to wrap it," she whispered. Sentences began to spill out jerkily.

"I wanted to buy a card. . . . I tried to. . . . I went into the store and bought one . . . but it was the wrong kind."

Choking back tears, she stumbled on.

"I didn't want to ask the man to read it to me. . . . I wanted to do it myself." She said she picked out a pretty card and rushed home to Edward to have him read it to her, only to discover that although the sentiments were appropriate, the card was written for a man to give a woman.

"I can't even buy a stupid card!" she cried out in despair.

We were silent as she struggled to control her emotions.

"But there's lots else you can do, Nicole," Matt said, finally. I reached back and took her hand.

His words seemed to take the edge off her misery. By the time we reached Dottie's parents' house, her eyes were dry. She climbed out of the car and slowly walked toward the party.

Matt turned off the car motor. We sat in silence watching as the door of the house opened into a brightly lighted room full of people. Nicole stepped inside, and the door closed behind her.

"How does she take it?" I cried. "Everywhere she turns, the world screams at her that she's inadequate. She's barred from all the fun that David and Jill enjoy. She's denied privileges they are given as a matter of course. She's excluded from the better paying, more interesting jobs. She's told she's too incompetent to have a baby—or at least I was harping on that until eight months ago. She can't even buy a card in a store without being mortified. No wonder she's despondent!"

Matt stared out the front window.

"And then," I continued, "we add to her problems. 'Go to work every day. Plan your time carefully. Eat right. Go to bed early. Clean your apartment. Budget your money. Use birth control.' That's what she hears from dawn to dusk. It's all so . . . rational, so middle class. Why does she have to live that way? Where is it written? Good God. She climbs mountains each day just to survive."

Matt looked at me. "So what are you saying?"

I shivered. "I guess I'm no longer sure I know what's best for her. There are many kinds of success. Maybe the best thing for her would be all-night sessions with friends, a baby or two, SSI for income—if she can get back on it—and a move to some place like Fremont."

He was incredulous. "Could you really accept that? An aimless life in which each day is lived for itself?"

Headlights from a passing car briefly lighted Matt's face, and then plunged it back into darkness.

"Yes, I think I could. Eight months ago, before I began this study, I would've shuddered at the thought. But I've changed."

Matt tapped his finger on the steering wheel. "It would mean less money . . . poorer health . . . being at the mercy of events rather than controlling them."

"I know, but I think it's where she's headed. Maybe not next year or the year after, but eventually. . . . "

He continued tapping his finger. After a minute, he started the car.

Smiles for an eighth-grade
graduation, 1973.

Enjoying macrame, age eighteen.

Wages and a uniform in 1976—
twenty-one-year-old Nicole had
landed her first job.

A mountain hike.

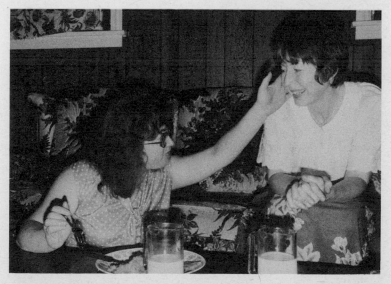

The night shift meant Nicole and Edward missed the family meal, but
Mom brought Thanksgiving plates to their apartment.

Nicole enjoying a moment with Edward.

Christmas holidays.

At last, a moped.

7

I don't know if
anyone loves me.

During the next six months bad luck and poor judgment combined to overwhelm Nicole and Edward. They almost overwhelmed me, too, because Nicole was now quite openly sharing their troubles—as long as Edward gave her permission to do so.

Matt and I learned the first piece of bad news when Edward stopped by to return a book on seashells.

"How's work going at Joey's?" I asked, as he handed it to Matt.

He looked down at his sneakers and turned his helmet slowly in his hands. "I got laid off," he whispered.

"Edward, I'm so sorry." Even though his modish glasses had a dark tint to them, we could tell he was fighting tears.

"Do you know why you lost it?" Matt asked gently.

"I was too slow. Also I was tardy and absent a lot. They said I was . . . " He struggled to think of the term used.

"Undependable?" Matt suggested.

"Yes, that's it." His shame was so acute, we quickly changed the subject.

Misfortune continued to dog him.

"Edward was in an accident. His moped is all smashed up," Nicole reported over the phone a few days later.

"What happened?"

She described the events that took place, as Edward revised each sentence of her version. Apparently he was riding behind a Datsun when it stopped and then suddenly backed up. It smashed into the front end of the moped which spun it, throwing Edward under the car.

"Is he okay?" I asked, tensely.

"Yeah. But the guy who was driving the Datsun— he wrote his insurance man's phone number on a piece of paper, and when I called it, the guy that answered was a shoe repairman."

I wanted to string the driver up by his toes.

"Did Edward, by any chance, get the license plate of the car?"

Nicole relayed my inquiry to Edward.

"No. I don't want to talk about it no more," he said. He'd been through enough for one day.

Two days later he pulled himself together enough to come to our house and get his bicycle out of our garage. It had been there since Christmas morning.

"Have you gotten an estimate for repairing the moped?" I asked.

"A hundred dollars," he said, his face impassively hiding his despair.

It was Nicole's turn to suffer adversity next. Somehow she managed to jab a piece of metal through her nail deep into her finger. She rode her moped to the clinic where her doctor numbed it and dug the offending piece out. But it became infected.

"How's your finger?" I asked, when I called her a week later. I'd been phoning her every day.

"It's okay. I've stopped taking the pain killer." She sounded less groggy than when she was taking the codeine, but she was discouraged.

"You'll continue taking the penicillin until it's all gone, won't you?"

"Yes."

"Good." (I'd discovered earlier that both she and Edward took antibiotics until they felt better and then shelved the remainder for a pick-me-up whenever one of them caught a cold.)

"I love you," I said, to cheer her up.

"<u>I don't know if anyone does</u> . . . ," she despaired.

While her finger was healing, Edward was dealt yet another blow. I learned about it over the phone when Nicole inadvertently mentioned that his thumb hurt.

"What's wrong with his thumb?" I asked.

"Can I tell her?" I heard her ask him, as she put her hand over the phone.

"He fell off my moped and broke his thumb," she said, when she removed her hand.

"When did this happen?"

"Last night when he got off work." (Although it had taken great courage to do so, Edward had returned to The Chowder Bowl on the 6:00 P.M. to 2:00 A.M. shift.) "He went to Emergency at the clinic, and they put it in a cast."

"How soon before he can go to work again?"

"Just a minute. I'll ask. Edward?"

All I could hear were the sounds of his karate show. Edward never missed "Kung Fu."

"Edward!"

("Ahhh! Unhhhhh!" Whap. "Eeeeeaaaah!" Whap.)

"EDWARD!"

(Whap. "Don't kill him"!) "What?" Edward grunted.

"How long did the doctor say before you can go to work?"

("Eeee oooh!" Whap. "Huh huh unf!" Whap.) "Three weeks. . . ."

Two weeks later they came to dinner. Nicole set the table while I did last minute cooking in the kitchen. Edward wandered in to see me.

"I sure am glad my cast is off," he said, hinting for attention.

I stopped everything and examined his thumb. It was grossly discolored and had a lump at the base.

"The doctor says the swelling will go down," he reassured me.

"How much is the doctor bill?" I asked, trying to keep the apprehension out of my voice.

"Three hundred dollars . . . so far," he said.

He left the kitchen, and I gripped the edge of the counter. Their lives were such a mess! I wanted to be able to "fix" it so they would be happier and not constantly in a state of crisis. But I didn't know what to do.

The next day I called Gordon. He had more bad news. "You're seeing only the tip of the iceberg," he said. "I can't tell you everything she reveals to me, but she calls me at least once a day. She begs for help with her problems, yet continues to ignore my suggestions— like closing that checking account. She's late every day for work and absent much too often. If I hadn't been on the phone talking with her Techtron supervisors regularly, she would have lost her job long ago."

I'd always known Gordon was one of Nicole's saints. Suddenly I realized the people at her work were, too. Their side had always been an unknown, because

Nicole had consistently refused to let me talk with them.

On top of everything else, Edward and Nicole went from illness to illness. Every bug that came along felled them because their resistance was so low.

And still they spent money as though they had a direct conduit to the United States Treasury.

"Could you, uh, bring Edward and me home from the rock concert?" she asked, when she called one evening.

"What rock concert?"

"The Foreigner. It's at the Forum. Tonight."

My blood pressure shot up eighty points. That money should go to the clinic and to Charlotte for her rent.

"How are you going to get there?" I asked, my voice barely containing my exasperation.

"By bus. But we don't think the buses run as late as 11:00 or 11:30."

I was too upset to care. "No. I'm sorry," I said. "I can't drive you home."

"That's okay," she said. She knew her request was an imposition. "We'll find a way back. No problem."

"Whaddya mean 'no problem'?" angrily demanded Edward in the background.

They arrived home by bus that night. Edward got busy with the bus schedules and found one running at 11:30.

I didn't know how the medical clinic was responding to their mounting bills, but I was aware of the strategies her grandmother had tried in her effort to extract Nicole's rent on the first of the month. Charlotte had provided Nicole with stamped, addressed envelopes; had taken Nicole to lunch on the first of the month; had met Nicole at work on the last payday of the month, and had arrived at Nicole's apartment every Friday night for weekly installments.

None of these methods worked, but Charlotte refused to give up. "If I kicked them out, they'd have to move to a neighborhood where it's not as safe," she stated obdurately. Charlotte was another of Nicole's saints.

One night I saw Gordon at a Go-Getters reunion. He broke into a chuckle when we greeted each other.

"What is it?" I asked.

"I can be downright sneaky at times. Last week I got together with Nicole and her Department of Rehab counselor, and we made Nicole sign a contract: 'Get up early (that means go to bed early) and get to Techtron on time—or you won't get driver training.'"

"So that's why I haven't heard Nicole mention the driver training lately. Is it working?"

"No, but there's always hope, isn't there?"

Nicole waltzed up. She played with Gordon's ear lobe and whispered something nonsensical. He smiled patiently. Then, spotting Roger coming in the door, she flew off to see him.

"Gordon," I said, "thank you for everything you're doing."

"It's nothing at all. I thrive on punishment," he said, as he turned to greet another parent.

One of the confidential matters I assumed that Nicole had discussed with Gordon was Edward. Things were not going well between them. It was understandable, considering all the strain they'd been under.

One evening Edward was walking on the beach, as he often did, and Nicole and I had some time alone together at her apartment. We wound up sitting on her bed. She was so relaxed, I thought it might be a good time to bring up the subject of matrimony.

"Do you know why Edward doesn't want to get married?" I asked. "I ask, because if he were your husband, he'd be covered by your medical insurance."

"He says he wants to have $1,000 in the bank, so he can buy a suit and rings and a honeymoon," she said, her eyebrows in the inverted "V" they assumed when she was distressed. "Sometimes he says he wants to be married by a 'free judge,' to get it over with, and then we can 'renew' it later. I tell him my mom would be hurt, if I did that. Would you be hurt?"

"Whatever you and Edward decide will be fine with me."

She began scratching at her wrist. "I want to go in for testing on why I can't get pregnant. Would you be happy to have a grandchild?"

"Of course," I fibbed, grateful that no baby had appeared to add still more stress to their lives. "I'd be concerned if it were handicapped, though."

"Me, too. I'd feel rotten. Edward would feel even more rotten."

We heard a key in the lock. "That's him!" she said, hopping off the bed. She greeted Edward at the door and pulled him into the bedroom. "Tell her about the wedding . . . " she urged, as she put her arms around him and nuzzled him.

"What wedding?"

"*Our* wedding."

He stiffened. Removing her arms as if she were a slimy octopus, he stalked into the bathroom.

"You don't want to have anything to do with me, do you?" she asked, plaintively, as she watched him go.

The door slammed behind him.

Day after day she called me in despair. She rarely

talked about her difficulties with Edward, but she kept me up to date on every illness and accident. In between, she wailed about never having enough money to buy the things she wanted.

Threading through this litany of complaints ran a curious preoccupation with the notion of "housewife." I was continually perplexed by it.

One day I began to understand what was going on.

"I've been pleading with Edward to let me stay home and be a housewife," she said when she called that day, "but he says I have to go to work."

"You're crazy to quit your job," Edward yelled from the other room. "It's a good job. You earn good money."

"Would Edward feel different about it if you were on SSI?"

"Just a minute. I'll see," she said, and left the phone. I couldn't hear what was said, but Nicole's voice was pleading, Edward's vehement.

"He'd be upset," she said, when she returned to the phone. "He says we can't afford it if I quit Techtron. But he doesn't realize how much I have to do when I get home from work. There's dishes, cooking supper, going to Safeway, having to go buy a birthday present, keeping the apartment clean. . . . I don't got any time hardly to get any rest."

Nicole had done an about-face, in recent months. She still had trouble getting to bed at a decent hour, but now it was because she was compulsively cleaning house. Everytime I went over there, the apartment was immaculate.

"Can't Edward help?"

"No. A man isn't supposed to do those things. The housewife is."

"But Nicole, you're not a housewife. You're a working woman, and Edward should help you."

"I'm a housewife! Just like you are!"

"I'm not one any longer," I started to argue. But suddenly I realized that having or not having a job wasn't the central issue. What was at stake was the status of "housewife" and all the associations that went with it. All her life she'd seen houses—in real life as well as on television—in which the mothers were at home. Like me, these women were surrounded by a husband, children, pretty furniture, kitchen appliances, and cars in the garage. When I told Nicole that she wasn't a housewife, I was stripping her of her right to this normal identification and to the possibility of having these things herself.

"Yes, dear, you're a housewife," I said. Her self-esteem was more important than Edward's sharing the work load.

She had another reason for wanting to stay home full-time. She never saw Edward. He was at work when she arrived home from Techtron and asleep when she got up the next morning. Their days off weren't even the same.

Her ingenuity was equal to that problem, though—at least temporarily. I found out about it by accident.

"If you won't let me stay home and be a housewife, could I work at The Chowder Bowl with you instead?" she asked Edward during another of her conversations with him while she had me on the phone line.

"No," shouted Edward. "The only reason they let you come last week was because someone was out sick."

That explained why she was "too sick" to go to Techtron the previous week.

"Please don't tell Daddy," she begged me, starting to cry.

"I won't, dear."

"Edward's so sweet and lovable," she whimpered, "and I never get to see him. I love working down there. Belle—she's the night manager—she's real nice. She likes me a lot." She began to sob. "I don't know what to do. I want to keep my job at Techtron. We got so many bills to pay. Do you have any opinion about what I should do?"

"I'm afraid I don't," I answered, sympathetically. My neutrality was genuine. I was as uncertain about the correct course of action as she was.

Life might be disappointing for her, but at least one thing was going right.

"Guess what! I'm starting driving lessons, and Rehab is paying for them," she exulted, when she dropped by on her way home from Techtron one evening.

I wasn't surprised. She hadn't fulfilled her part of the contract that Gordon and the Rehab counselor had made her sign, but I'd known all along they'd cave in. Given enough time, she could have talked them into underwriting skydiving lessons.

"When does the instruction begin?"

"In two weeks. Then, as soon as I get my license, I'll be able to borrow one of your cars when I have errands to do."

I faced her squarely. "Nicole, you are not going to use our cars."

"Okay, then Daddy will buy me a car."

"Your father is not, do you hear me, is *not* going to buy you a car." An upsetting wave of *déjà vu* swept over me.

On May first, two weeks later, Matt, Jill, and I heard a horn honking in the alley. It was so insistent, I investigated and then called the others to come.

There sat Nicole at the wheel of a large car with a yellow sign, "California Driving School," glowing on the top.

Her instructor, an amiable gentleman, jumped out to meet us. Explaining that his specialty was teaching the handicapped to drive, he opened Nicole's door to show us the steering knob, and the hand-operated brakes and accelerator.

"Nicole doesn't use this equipment, of course," he said. "It's for paraplegics and people who've had strokes."

"Does it have automatic transmission?" Matt asked, leaning over Nicole to see the equipment.

"Oh, yes. She uses that. It would be too difficult for her to learn to drive with a stick shift." Matt straightened up and shut the door, and we all pondered the phenomenon of Nicole at the steering wheel of a car.

The object of our consideration looked nervous.

"How's she doing?" we asked the instructor.

"She tends to go a little too slow sometimes, and she gets annoyed when someone hugs her rear, but she's learning." He grinned at her.

She swallowed hard. "Can I go around the block and come back?"

"Sure," he said, and climbed back into the passenger seat next to her.

Matt, Jill, and I watched while Nicole started the engine. The car began to move slowly down the alley, its driver gripping the wheel with terror. It disappeared around the corner, and we began to wait.

Three minutes went by—then five. Jill gave up and went back into the house. Finally, the yellow-lighted sedan crept around the corner at the other end of the alley.

"I didn't know if she was going to return or not, she went so many blocks," her instructor said.

Matt and I waved them good-bye, and Nicole again eased slowly down the alley.

"I'll bet you were real proud of me last night," Nicole said, when she called the next day. "I need to practice driving on my own time, though. Do you have any suggestions on how I could do that?"

"None whatsoever," I answered.

"Oh."

"Nicole, how are you going to use your driving skills, if you do pass the test? You can't afford a car, and we're not going to buy you one."

"Daddy said he would if me and Edward moved to Lemon Grove."

True, in an unguarded moment, he had said that. After Nicole had glowingly described to us the 101st apartment that "costed only eight hundred" and asked why she couldn't move there, Matt had explained that one arrangement she could afford, other than her present one, might be a mobile home placed on one of our orange ranches near Lemon Grove. Nicole had pressed him: if she lived out in the country like that, wouldn't she have to have a car? Matt finally admitted she would.

"But that's for Lemon Grove," I said. "Do you really want to move there?" She had been rather bored the once or twice she had accompanied us on our trips north to confer with Osamu Takeda, our farm manager and close friend.

"I don't know. But I can get 'reproduced' cars through the driving school."

I thought a minute. "'Repossessed' cars?"

"Yeah. I can get them for $600 off because I'm a pupil. I want to talk with Daddy about buying me one . . . for Lemon Grove."

My head began to ache.

"Edward doesn't want to learn to drive right now,"

she continued. "Too much on his mind. . . ."

I hung up the phone and took an aspirin.

In mid-May, two weeks later, Nicole phoned. "I passed!" she yelled.

"Congratulations," I said, mustering what little enthusiasm I could.

"Can I borrow the 'bus' to take my friends to Disneyland?" she asked, without stopping for breath. She meant our Volkswagen camper. It was the only one of our cars that had an automatic transmission.

"No."

"I thought you'd say that," she said. She wasn't angry. It was more like she was biding her time.

In early June, Matt took Edward and Nicole up to Lemon Grove for the weekend. The countryside was at its most beautiful. Row upon row of green crops and ripening fruit trees whirled past the car windows, and the heavy sweetness of freshly mowed alfalfa filled the air.

Nicole took on the role of guide to Edward the Tourist during the three-hour trip, his first excursion north.

"That's peach trees," she instructed Edward as they passed a walnut grove.

"Daddy's ranch is that big," she said grandly, when they drove past a thousand-acre farm.

"Not quite," Matt said, explaining that our land lay in a few ten- and twenty-acre plots.

In Lemon Grove, after Matt had completed his business with Osamu, he took Edward and Nicole to a sales lot for used mobile homes and trailers. Nicole inspected the portable housing with interest, but her attention was focused on the return home: Matt had promised she could drive part of the way.

"She was extremely cautious," Matt told me, as he unlaced his dusty boots on their return. "At one point she was indecisive about whether to go through or brake for a yellow light, and I had to lecture her, but other than that, she did okay. I told her we'd never feel safe letting her drive in the city, though."

Nicole either didn't hear the last part, or chose to ignore it. "Can you let me take the 'bus' so I can practice my driving?" she begged the next day, and the next, and the next.

"Nicole—I would have to go with you, and I have my seminars, my work at UCLA, my housework. . . . I'm just too busy."

"I don't want to 'hurt' you and Daddy, but can I tell you something? I don't think it's fair you let David and Jill drive alone, but you have to be with me when I drive."

I tried to think of a response.

She didn't want one. "See, I hate to take you away from the things you need to do. The only reason I want to drive alone is to save you time."

Yeah. Right, I thought to myself.

In June she had to deal with what she viewed as a minor irritation.

"Mother, what does c-o-l-l-e-c-t-i-o-n-a-g-e-n-c-y spell?"

I wasn't surprised at this news, either. I'd been expecting it for months.

" 'Collection agency.' Who sent you the notice?"

"The clinic. They sent it to Edward. What does it mean? Is it bad?"

"If Edward's bills have gone to a collection agency,

that's not good. But I ought to see the notice before I say any more. How about I come over and take a look at it?"

"Well . . . uh. . . . " She covered the phone with her hand, and I heard a muffled conversation with Edward.

"Edward said it was okay to tell you about the car," she said, removing her hand, " 'cause you'll see it if you come over. We rented a car."

"Oh?" I said, trying to sound calm.

"It's so beautiful," she cooed. "Just the kind we want to buy—a Toyota Corolla."

"How nice. When did you get it?"

"Wednesday."

"I'll be there in a few minutes."

The second I arrived at their apartment, Nicole hustled me back down the stairs. She unlocked the garage door, lifted it up—I could almost hear the drum roll—and there, by gum, sat a Toyota Corolla.

"Come see the inside," she squealed, as she opened the car door. As I was clearly going to be allowed no peace until the interior was inspected, I sat down in the driver's seat and commented favorably on the decor.

"How come there's popcorn all over the floor?" I asked, standing up and unkinking my back.

"Everybody went to a drive-in movie last night. We had a super time."

"That sounds like fun. How much is the rental?"

"Twenty-four dollars a day plus gas," she stated, a little uneasily, and then added, "It'll be returned tomorrow."

That would be ninety-six dollars, plus gas. Amazing.

As she locked the garage door, two boys in swimming trunks rattled past us on their skateboards. The annual trek of the bathing suit crowd to the beach had begun, even though we were having our usual overcast

June weather.

"Hi, Mrs. Kaufman," Shelley said. She was standing at the top of the stairs with a Walkman set plugged into her ears. Shelley had recently moved in with Nicole and Edward.

"Daddy brought my things over last weekend," Shelley told me, as I took a quick glance around the apartment. The only indication anyone had been added was a small bureau in the corner of the bedroom.

"Where's your bed?" I asked.

"On the floor of the living room," Nicole informed me. "That's why Edward and I have ordered a couch."

I dropped into one of the wicker chairs.

"It's a sleeper couch, queen size," Nicole continued. "Don't worry. We're not getting it on credit. We paid cash for it. The owner of the shop is real nice. He likes me a lot."

"How much did you give him?" I asked, dreading the answer.

"Seven hundred dollars—our income tax money."

"Do you have a receipt?"

"I think so. . . . " She began rummaging in a desk drawer. Papers were extracted and examined, to little effect.

"Do you promise me," I asked, finally, "that if you have any trouble getting that couch, you'll let me know?"

"Yes, Momma. But I go in there everyday and tell him he better hurry up with it."

Somehow I felt better. In fact, I almost began to feel sorry for the shop owner.

Edward, by this time, had emerged from the bedroom with the notice from the clinic in his hand. He stood, waiting, while I read it. Nicole did, too. Shelley had sprawled on the orange bean-bag chair, lost in the music provided by her Walkman.

"You're in luck, Edward," I said. "This is just a warning. It says your bill will be sent to a collection agency if you don't start paying off the $368 you owe for your thumb."

Edward shifted from one foot to the other. "Is a collection agency bad?"

"Yes, it is. You could have trouble from then on charging anything—including medical services."

He blanched.

"They don't understand our situation," Nicole snorted. "I'm going to the clinic right now and explain it to them. Will you take us?" she asked, turning to me.

"I could, but they won't be interested. All they want is your money."

Edward seemed highly dubious about confronting anyone at the clinic under those circumstances, but Nicole was already starting out the door. "We're going to straighten this thing out," she said.

Suddenly she stopped. "I can drive us over there!"

I had seen it coming and had been helpless. "I suppose you can," I sighed. "But you'll drive the camper, not the Toyota." I felt more in control in my own car.

Nicole grabbed the car keys out of my purse and ran out the door. Edward and I followed her down the stairs, leaving Shelley listening to her tunes.

Nicole unlocked the camper and hoisted herself up onto the driver's seat. Edward climbed into the back. I stayed up front next to Nicole.

We didn't move for eight minutes. Nicole adjusted the seat for her short legs. Then she adjusted the side rearview mirror. The rearview mirror over the dash. The rearview mirror by my window, an exercise that required climbing over my lap three times. Having completed her fine-tuning, she went to work on the seat belt. She finally had to give up on lengthening it, but not before she'd chastised me thoroughly for imprudently owning a vehicle with seatbelts that couldn't be adjusted.

Finally she started the car and began the drive to the clinic, a distance of two miles. Her speed was still dangerously slow, but the terror was gone. It had been replaced by smugness. At one point as she tooled along, she insisted I bend toward her so she could kiss me on the cheek.

When we arrived, she parked the camper, and marched into the building. Edward and I trailed behind her.

"I'm Nicole Kaufman," she announced.

"Yes?" the woman at the front desk said.

"I've come about my bill," Nicole said, irked that the lady didn't know why she was there.

"Straight ahead into that office," the woman directed.

We all filed in that direction. Patients in the waiting room looked at Nicole. She was barefoot, bra-less, and had on shorts topped by a tight T-shirt labeled "Shake Your Booty."

In the Business Office, Nicole repeated her message. She also handed the receptionist Edward's statement.

"Please have a seat. Your representative will call you in a moment."

As soon as I'd settled myself with a magazine, a young woman appeared at the door and asked, "Nicole Kaufman?"

Nicole jumped up and followed her through the Business Office and into her cubicle. Edward and I shuffled after them.

Nicole, arms waving, gushed out her version of the

bill problem.

The young woman listened, but she kept looking at Edward's statement. "The name on this statement is Brichant, not Kaufman . . . " she said, perplexed.

"My name isn't changed yet," Nicole explained.

"Oh. Just a minute." The young woman called another employee into the cubicle. "Which representative should this patient see about changing her name?"

"See, I've been paying on my bill, but my name isn't Brichant yet," Nicole continued, smiling encouragingly. "I sent a check last week."

The two women studied Nicole. They called another woman. Gradually, after they'd asked Nicole innumerable questions, they figured out that she had nothing to do with the bill. It was the quiet young man behind her whose statement was in question. With that point settled, the representative who handled "A through E" patients took over, and we filed into her cubicle.

Nicole chortled, enjoying to the utmost the attention she was receiving.

In the new cubicle, the "A through E" woman began tapping on the keyboard of her computer terminal. Edward's record soon rolled down the green screen in ominous white letters and numbers.

"The numbers in the far right column are in the last stage of delinquency," she pointed out. Most of Edward's "numbers" were on view there.

"What's 'delinquency'?" Nicole asked.

The lady began explaining. Nicole and Edward tried to understand, but their eyes soon dulled.

"Delinquency means 'bad,' " I interjected, having decided we were going to be there all day, if I didn't.

"Would you like to begin a payment schedule?" the young woman asked Edward. "It will have to be a large amount, because you owe $448. You've had some doctor visits since the last statement was sent."

He looked at me to translate.

"Would you like to pay a certain amount each month—say $50—toward your bill?" I said.

He audibly gulped and nodded.

"Then I'll have to go get a yellow form," the woman said, excusing herself.

"And you always talk about buying a car," Edward growled at Nicole.

The "A through E" woman returned, and the forms were completed and signed.

"You're nice," Nicole said to her, as we turned to leave. "Can I come see you if I have problems with my bill?"

"No, you should see the first lady you met. She handles 'F through K.'"

Nicole was disappointed. "I see. 'Cause my name isn't Mrs. Brichant yet. I wish it were changed already. . . ." She looked wistfully at Edward. He squirmed.

The ride back to their apartment, although Nicole took the longest route that could possibly be devised, was a quiet one. I sensed it was not the time for chatter, so I remained silent.

At one point, though, I spoke up. Nicole had pulled into a left turn lane without a traffic light, and sat waiting for the oncoming traffic to let up.

"Nicole, what does that say?" I asked her, pointing to a sign straight ahead.

She hadn't even noticed it. "'No . . . left . . . turn,'" she read. She took a second to digest what she'd read—and looked at me with alarm.

"What else does the sign say?" I asked.

"'Between?'" (She wasn't certain she'd read the word correctly.) "'four and six?'" She turned to me, eyes wide. "It's okay to turn between four and six?"

"No. The sign reads 'No left turn between 4 and 6 P.M., Sundays and holidays excepted.'"

Her bewilderment was acute. An opening in the traffic had arrived, and she wanted clear cut instructions, not D.M.V. trafficalese.

"You can turn," I said. She heaved an enormous sigh and did so.

But I was concerned. Safe driving included being able to read signs and understand them. How was she going to manage? I was still stewing over the folly of the D.M.V. in giving her a license, when she pulled the camper up at her door.

"Oh, I almost forgot," I said, as she started to get out. "I've made our yearly dental appointment for the family, and, as always, you're included, if you want to join us."

Nicole looked accusingly back at Edward. "He should come, too. He never brushes his teeth."

"I do, too," he protested.

"Lately you been doing it every day, but before, you weren't doing it. Right?"

Edward sat like a stone.

"Okay, that 'before' could've affected cavities." Edward jerked his lower jaw back and forth sideways. He'd begun doing that lately.

"Well," I said brightly, "maybe one day he'll join us, but now I've got to get home." I gave Nicole a kiss, and they both climbed out. As I turned the corner, I saw Nicole waving. Edward had fled up the stairs.

8

*Seems like I'm learning
to live alone
the hard way.*

At age twenty-four, Nicole had little reason to fear the dentist. While the rest of us lined up to have our cavities filled, she was given a clean bill of health, just as she had been all the other years.

After that triumph, she and Edward were plunged into more calamities.

Edward's moped was stolen. He'd finally had it repaired, and had begun riding it to work at The Chowder Bowl. But one night when he went to get it at the bike rack, it was gone. The chain had been cut. Grief stricken, he called the police, but they gave him little hope of seeing it again.

He and Nicole fell for a bunco scheme. When they received a mail invitation to save money by joining a buyers' club, they signed up. Nicole said they drove "out there" and gave "somebody" $100. After a few days, they reconsidered and tried to get their money back, but the swindlers had vanished.

They left themselves open to thievery. One eve-

157

ning when Nicole was home alone, a neighbor came in to use the phone. While he was there, he asked for a drink of water. She left the room to get it. Five minutes after he'd gone, Nicole discovered their rent money— $300 in cash—was missing. It had been lying next to the phone. She angrily confronted the neighbor in his home, but he denied having taken it.

"Seems like I'm learning to live alone the hard way," she despaired, as each of these experiences unfolded.

She *was* learning, though. The reason the rent payment was in bills was because she'd closed the checking account. That was growth—except now she and Edward were more vulnerable to theft because they were working with cash.

I didn't know whether to cheer or weep. Much of the time I didn't care. I just wanted to get off the phone. Each time it rang, Nicole was at the other end reporting a new catastrophe. Or, if none had occurred in the past four hours, she wanted to "talk," her euphemism for stewing endlessly over whether she should quit her job.

Or she would explain all the reasons why she simply had to borrow the camper *now*.

"Hi," she started in. It was her third call that day.

"We're eating," I said. "May I call you back in fifteen minutes?"

"Yeah, but can I ask you a question?"

"I suppose so," I said, wearily. "What is it?"

"Can I use the camper?"

"No."

"But I need to get my groceries from Dottie's. See, some of the food needs to go in the refrigerator."

While my meal got progessively colder, she explained why the groceries were at Dottie's, where Dottie lived, why she would only be home between 7:15 and

7:45, which bag contained the perishables. . . .

By the time I got off the phone, I was foaming at the mouth. Matt went to get the groceries.

I was a little more patient when she fretted about whether she should leave Techtron or not. That was a real Catch 22. If she quit, she'd lose the income and the benefits, and incur the wrath of her father and Edward. If she remained there, she'd never see Edward, and she'd have to continue doing work she hated.

One day an opportunity to resolve her conflict appeared. She took advantage of it—but not without suffering a sizable dose of guilt.

"Where'd you get those?" I asked, when she arrived at our house wearing black kewpie-shaped spectacles.

"I went down to the ocean to test the water, and a big wave knocked me down." The spectacles were temporary ones given her by the optometrist, she explained. Her new glasses wouldn't be ready for another three weeks.

"Can you see well enough to go to work?"

"No. Here's the Tupperware bowl I borrowed. I can't stay because the car is. . . . " She caught herself and stopped.

"Have you rented another car?"

"I don't want to talk about it," she snapped, and stalked out the door. I could hear a car running in the alley.

Matt was suspicious when he learned what had happened. He tried to avoid confronting her, but two weeks later, when he realized she was not at work, his restraint crumbled.

"Are your glasses ready yet?" he asked her during one of her phone calls.

"No."

"Have you talked to the people at your work

lately?"

There was a long pause. "Yes. . . . "

"What did they say?"

"They called me Monday."

"Are you fired?"

"Yes," she whispered. "I . . . I didn't want to tell you."

"Were you surprised?" he demanded, his voice rising.

"No . . . "

"You could've gone to work with those glasses, you know."

"No, I couldn't! I couldn't see. I still can't see," she protested.

"You're playing games with me, Nicole. How come you were able to drive that car?"

No answer.

"How come?"

Still no answer.

"Here," he said, thrusting the phone at me.

"Nobody believes me!" Nicole cried in my ear. "Daddy doesn't. Edward doesn't. My boss doesn't." Over and over she insisted she was a victim of circumstances.

"I know, dear," I kept saying until her protests died down. When she no longer felt the need to defend herself, she began to detail her plans for her new freedom. She was going to collect SSI and spend her time making concoctions in her crock-pot, sewing curtains for the bedroom, taking a bus up to Lemon Grove to see if she'd like to live there . . .

"Wait a minute," I cautioned. "Maybe you won't be able to get SSI."

"Oh." She knew that was a possibility but had conveniently forgotten it.

"You know where the Social Security office is. Go see if you can talk them into funding you again."

A few days later she showed up with application papers. I completed them, and she disappeared again.

"The lady said I can't get it anymore," she reported with disgust the following week. I read the letter in her hand. It stated that Nicole was no longer considered handicapped because she'd been employed too long.

And that was that. Her mental retardation had been wiped out by bureaucratic fiat.

But her disabilities hadn't. That was abundantly clear when I went with her to the Department of Employment to help her file for unemployment compensation.

I directed Nicole to a window where a claims representative handed her a form, and we sat down at a large table to complete it. Other applicants joined us. They took twenty minutes or so to fill in their forms, and left. We were there for three hours.

"No," I instructed, "not in that space. In this one. Write 't' . . . 'h' . . . 'e' . . . Now leave room. No, not that much room. Okay, now write 'c' . . . 'h' . . . 'o' . . . 'w' . . . 'd' . . . No, no, no. You've made a 'b.' The bump faces the other way on a 'd.' "

"Like this?" She drew a correct "d" on the margin of the form.

"Yes."

She hunched over, jerkily scratched at the offending bump, and fashioned a correct one. She looked up. Suddenly her chin jutted forward and she peered at my eyes. "Why do you have those funny curved things in your glasses?"

"They're bifocals. Now leave another space. Write real small. You haven't much room left."

"What are bifocals?"

"I'll tell you later. Write 'e.'"

Her eyes drifted to my button-down collar. "Did you know you got a button missing?"

"Yes. Write 'e.' "

She reached up to inspect the detached point of my collar, but became distracted by her nails. "You like my polish?" Dangling her hand in front of me, she displayed the poison red she'd applied.

"It's lovely. Write 'e'."

"Boy, you really get in a hurry, don't you?" She picked up her pen again. "Okay, 'e' . . . "

" 'r' . . . Leave a space. New word. 'b' . . . 'o' . . . 'w' . . . 'l.' "

The "bowl" was so large it took up the spaces where her dates of employment and wages were supposed to be entered.

"Your next appointment will be at 11:00 A.M. on Tuesday," the claims representative informed her, after he'd looked over her completed application.

"Better make it 2:00 P.M.," she suggested. Maybe she couldn't read or write, but she knew her sleep cycle. She missed the appointment anyway. And the rescheduled one. But she made it to the third one, brought home more papers for us to complete, returned them to the Employment office, and was rewarded with unemployment compensation.

"Dottie has food stamps. Where do I go to get those?" she asked, a week later.

I wanted to scream, "I don't have time! I have all I can do just to keep up with your phone calls!"

"Why don't you ask Gordon to help you get them?" I squeaked. She called him and then phoned me back. "He can't. He just got ten new clients."

I drove her to the Department of Social Services, and she was enrolled in the food stamps program.

"Mom, if I go back there, I can get Medi-Cal," Nicole said ten days later. "Penny has Medi-Cal, and she says you get it at that same office."

"But you don't have to take me," she added quickly, sensing that my neural circuits had hit overload. "I'll go by bus—even though it takes me all day, and I could do it real fast if you lent me the camper."

Shelley went with her. Edward was making too much money to be eligible for Medi-Cal, but Shelley had only a part-time job at a convalescent home, and Nicole had decided her friend should apply. The night before they left, I rounded up Nicole's birth certificate, made sure she had her Social Security number, and enlisted Matt's help for two hours while we sorted through Edward's and her pay stubs (they'd been thrown in a drawer together) to figure out which were Nicole's and then to set aside those covering the past two months.

"Did you get it?" I asked Nicole when she called that night to report.

"Yup. No problem. Now I can have my arm taken care of." She'd had a small irritation in her armpit, and I'd told her to stop using deodorant, but she forgot. It was becoming increasingly tender.

"How about Shelley?" I asked. "Did she get it, too?"

"Not yet, 'cause she told the lady she isn't handicapped."

"I'm not handicapped," Shelley protested to Edward in the background. "I'm not handicapped."

"In a way you are," Nicole reflected. "You were in the retarded class with me in school."

"I didn't belong there! My daddy kept trying to take me out, but they insisted."

"Being retarded," Edward instructed the two women patiently, "isn't the same as being handicapped.

Handicapped is, like, when you have a fake leg, or you're in a wheelchair."

Nicole thought a minute. "But I got Medi-Cal today because I checked 'handicapped' on the card, and that's 'cause I'm retarded."

What Nicole said was true. This was a knottier problem than Edward had thought. How could he solve the semantics yet preserve Shelley's self-esteem?

"Maybe being retarded is like being a little bit handicapped?" he admitted.

Shelley saw no practical purpose in such fine distinctions. "How am I going to get Medi-Cal?"

"Here, talk with my mom," Nicole said, somehow confident I would have a solution. Shelley took the phone.

"You could continue to tell them you're not handicapped," I suggested to her. "Just say you were in classes for the retarded when you were in school."

"Oh. Okay."

Shelley got her Medi-Cal coverage.

Nicole tried to put hers to work immediately. By then the lump under her arm was "puffy and red and sort of blue," but when she went to her clinic, the receptionist told her it didn't accept Medi-Cal patients. The nearest doctor who did was seven miles away. She couldn't call me because I was out of town, so she went home.

In the middle of the night, she was in such pain that she rode her moped to the Emergency Room at a nearby hospital. There a doctor numbed the area and lanced the infection—"I saw him do the whole thing," she told us later; "a whole lot of stuff came out"—and sent her home with instructions to see her own doctor the next day.

"What did he say?" I asked her the following evening, after she'd seen her regular doctor at the clinic.

"He said it's coming along real good. He gave me some penicillin."

Two days later, her report was far less rosy.

"My arm's sore. I've been throwing up all day. I'm all hot and cold."

"Are you taking the penicillin?"

"No. Edward went to get it, but he came back without it because he didn't have enough money."

"Let me speak to Edward."

He took the phone. After two or three minutes of quizzing, I realized that it was the Emergency Room doctor who had prescribed the antibiotic. That was three days ago.

I dashed to the pharmacy where Edward had left the prescription, scooped up the medicine, and rushed to their apartment. By that time Edward had left for work.

"Who's there?" Nicole called, when I knocked.

"Your mother." Even in my agitated state, I was impressed by her caution.

She opened the door. Standing there in her old flannel nightgown and matted hair, she looked the picture of misery.

While she crept back into bed, I went to get her a glass of water in the kitchen.

"Oh, I see your new couch has come," I called, as I walked through the living room. "Doesn't it look pretty."

She staggered to her feet and leaned against the bedroom doorway. "It took four men to get it through the door."

The queen-sized sleeper in orange and brown flowered velvet took up a quarter of the room. New end tables, each supporting a large amber glass lamp, sat on either side of the couch. One lamp was minus a shade.

"We got that one on sale," she explained, as I led her back to bed.

"Here's the first pill," I said, handing her the water. "Be sure you take all of them now."

Within a few days she was better, and her arm was healing nicely.

Two weeks later The Chowder Bowl called her to come in and work for a few nights because an employee was out sick. When she rode home the first night, it was raining, and the moped slipped as she turned a corner. She fell. Her helmet protected her head, but she painfully bruised her shoulder.

"Do you think I should go to work?" she asked me the next day shortly before she was due to leave.

"Does it hurt to move your arm?"

"Yes."

"I'd stay home. You lift some pretty heavy things down there."

"You have to go to work," I heard Edward insisting, "or we can't pay the rent."

She went with him. But she called me later in the evening from home.

"I got burned. I was carrying a pot of chili, and it slipped in my hands."

"Good heavens. Where are you burned?"

"Across my face. The chili splattered. I put some ice on it right away."

I hurried to her apartment. A raw area about the size of a silver dollar had been gouged in her cheek. Around it and on her arms were smaller burns. The thought of the scar the large one could leave, especially if she picked at the scab, made me weak.

"You promise not to dig at it as it heals?"

"I'll try not to."

She sat despondently on the bed. I sat down beside

her and put my arm around her. "My friends all say I'm so lucky to have such nice parents. . . . "

"Oh?" I said. A warm glow began spreading from the pit of my stomach. "What do you mean by 'lucky'?"

"Their parents don't buy them cars and mobile homes in the country. . . . " With that introduction, she launched into a full-blown description of the amenities she and Edward would enjoy when they moved to Lemon Grove. This particular version included not only a car and a mobile home, but also a dog, a vegetable garden, fruit trees from which she would pick peaches to make—and sell—jam, and a hot tub. And a horse in a stable.

At least she has her fantasies, I thought. Thank God for that.

The setbacks continued. Her moped was vandalized at the bike rack near The Chowder Bowl. Someone applied a blowtorch to the chain, and, finding it impervious, settled for slashing the tires and melting the turn signals.

Her billfold was stolen. She left her purse, open, in her grocery cart as she shopped, and when she got to the check-out stand, she discovered her wallet was missing —with fifty dollars, her driver's license, and her bus pass.

A thief took Edward's bicycle. Edward left it unlocked while he and Nicole ate in a restaurant. When he went to retrieve it, it was gone.

Nevertheless, the burn healed, miraculously, without leaving a scar. Nicole resolved to keep her purse over her shoulder in the supermarket. And Edward decided bikes had better be locked up, even at restaurants.

Although they were continuing to learn "the hard

way," some knowledge they picked up painlessly. At a party we gave for David when he was leaving for graduate school, Matt manned the blender making daiquiris while Nicole watched.

"I like strawberry daiquiris best," she commented.

"You do? Where have you had those?" Matt asked.

"At Tequila Pete's. We go there all the time. But I make them myself at home."

She had learned about beer, too, Jill discovered when she and Nicole went grocery shopping for David's party. As Jill tried to decide which kind to buy, Nicole advised, "Budweiser has more 'head' than Coors. And we better get the 'shorts.' Beer gets warm before you finish a 'tall.'"

Jill nearly fell over the beer display. "Do you drink beer?"

"No. I don't like it."

Jill poked her in the ribs. "I'll bet. Don't you drink it just a teeny weeny bit?"

"No. I don't like it." She said it so ingenuously that Jill concluded Edward or their friends must be the beer drinkers.

She discovered that Nicole knew a few other things about shopping in a supermarket. She exchanged the small bags of frozen peas that Jill had thrown into the cart for large ones, because they were less expensive. She inspected the dates on dairy items. She knew which were the cheaper brands of canned goods.

But she had trouble with the lettering in produce signs. "Are these that price?" she asked Jill. She held two boxes of cherry tomatoes in her hands while she studied a card that read "Radishes: 2 for 35¢."

"No. It's for the radishes."

"Where's the price for these then?"

Jill pointed to it off at one side: "Box tomatoes:

$1.25 each."

Wide-eyed, Nicole replaced the tomatoes.

She also had weaknesses, which Jill was quick to point out. A box of doughnuts tempted Nicole so badly that her fingers twitched.

"You don't need those," Jill said, patting her sister's generous stomach.

"You got your Fruit Loops!"

Jill flushed. "That's different. Besides, I'll give you some, okay?"

David's party was a resounding success—the "shorts" stayed cold—and he prepared to leave for the East Coast on Sunday morning.

"Please come down to The Chowder Bowl Saturday night," Nicole begged. She'd be working there that weekend. "It'll be the last time I get to see you."

"You bet," David promised. He and his girlfriend would drop by after dinner.

I woke David at 7:00 Sunday morning. "Did you see Nicole?" I asked. "She kept calling all evening saying you hadn't gotten there yet."

He covered his squeezed eyes with a hand from under the sheets and groaned. "Oh, Christ. I forgot. . . . "

Throwing back the covers, he tore down the stairs to call her. On the couch sat Matt comforting a sobbing Nicole. She was in her blue nylon uniform top and stained white trousers. Her shoulder-length hair was tangled from being slept on.

David took Matt's place.

"You didn't come," she cried disconsolately. "I wanted to see my brother before he left."

"I know, Nicole. I'm so sorry." He hugged and stroked her.

"When did she get here?" I asked Matt, when he came back upstairs to get dressed.

"She said she worked until 3:00 A.M., rode her moped here, let herself in with her key, and went to sleep on the couch."

While we dressed and David brought his luggage downstairs, Nicole combed her hair, put it up in its twist, and changed into clean trousers. On the way to the airport she clung to him, occasionally putting her head on his shoulder. Even at the airport, she did so. When he finally succeeded in separating himself from her, she ran to the terminal window to watch him stride across the tarmac.

She recovered quickly, however. On the way home, she quizzed Jill about her new boyfriend, criticized Matt's driving, and told us about a fight that had broken out the night before in front of The Chowder Bowl. That reminded her of something.

"Belle has asked me to work full-time," she said. "Ramón has to go back to Mexico. He got a letter, and his wife is real bad sick."

Nicole had told me how hard Ramón worked to be able to send money home. I felt sorry for him, but I was elated that Nicole had been offered his position. Although it paid only entry-level wages, that was more than she was getting on unemployment.

"Are you going to take it?" I asked, detecting she had some misgivings about the proposal. ·

"I don't know. We need the money real bad. But Edward—see, he likes me taking care of him. He doesn't want me to go back to work."

Matt turned off the beach road and started up the hill toward our house. "You don't really have a choice," he said. "If the people at the Department of Employment found out you turned down a job, they'd cut off your funds."

"Oh."

That settled that. Nicole joined the night crew of The Chowder Bowl that evening.

The frequency of her phone calls decreased dramatically. Except for her days off, she went to work at 6:00 P.M., got off sometime between 2:00 and 4:00 A.M., and slept until mid-afternoon the next day. A schedule like that allowed little time for phone conversations.

But when she did call, she often spoke of how proud she was of her contribution at The Chowder Bowl. "We're a real good crew," she declared. "Belle doesn't have to tell us what to do. Me and Edward and Connie and Juan—we just know."

I had difficulty weighing economic security against satisfaction like that.

After she'd been working there a month, Matt and I decided we'd drop by. We hadn't been to The Chowder Bowl since Nicole and Daniel Gold, the man who had originally hired her, had squared off.

We strolled down one evening. Not much had changed. The brightly lighted pier area still looked like a cross between Coney Island and Waikiki Beach with its open air restaurants, amusement park rides for children, and Hawaiian clothing outlets. There were fewer people now, though, because it was fall.

Matt and I stationed ourselves back from the food stand far enough that Nicole would be unlikely to see us but our view of the counter would be good. We were, however, too far away to be able to hear her.

Edward was immediately visible. In his blue baseball cap with "Chowder Bowl" written across it and his blue nylon shirt, he moved back and forth taking and filling orders through the din of the sizzling fryers and thumping rock band in the Tiki Tiki Bar next door. Nicole was nowhere to be seen.

Suddenly her head popped up in a "window" in the

array of hanging pots and pans behind him. Her hair was hidden under a kerchief. She called to him, and they exhanged some sort of work-related information. He returned to his customers. Her head disappeared.

Shortly afterward, she swung around the corner into full view. She checked the fryers, prepared two hamburgers that she took off the grill (she put *two* slices of pickle on the plates), stirred a pot of chili, and lifted the lid off a vat of steaming corn. Seeing it needed resupplying, she traveled to the end of the counter and returned with fresh ears which she dropped into the steamer. While she was doing this, Edward and two other uniformed young men—one chubby, the other thin—were calling orders to her.

Returning to the grill, she began filling them: two fish plates, three hamburgers, a ham and cheese sandwich, and a corn dog. No one would have awarded her a prize for speed, but her movements were smooth and thoroughly professional. How proud Daniel Gold would have been.

"I can't believe it," Matt breathed.

"Neither can I." For ten minutes we watched.

"Let's go say hello," he said finally. As we walked toward the counter, Edward saw us and tapped Nicole on her shoulder. She finished plunging a fryer loaded with raw potato sticks into the snapping fat, set the timer, and turned around.

"How do you remember all those orders?" Matt asked, grinning at her.

"Oh, I dunno. I just do." Another order was called, and she stopped to listen. "Sometimes I forget, though, and then I go ask." She wiped some perspiration off her forehead with the back of her hand. "I gotta go," she said. Matt and I could see we were distracting her.

"Okay, sweetheart," Matt said. "We'll just have a

cup of coffee and walk on home."

Matt purchased our coffee and we moved toward one of the redwood tables. I was just sitting down when Matt grabbed my arm.

"Look," he said.

I looked back at the counter in time to see the chubby employee leer at Nicole and give her a push with his hip.

"Cut it out," barked Nicole without looking at him. She bent across the grill to scrape it. He gazed at her protruding bottom and smirked deliciously at the thin employee. His buddy grinned. Glancing to satisfy himself that Belle wasn't in sight, the plump youth bumped into Nicole again, this time spilling Coke across her rear end.

"Oh, I'm so sorry," he taunted. He and his friend guffawed in delight. Nicole didn't even acknowledge their existence.

I jerked to my feet. HOW DARE YOU! I wanted to yell. DON'T YOU REALIZE THIS WOMAN HAS ACHIEVED A MIRACLE?

But I said nothing. Neither did Matt. We both just died a little inside. Somehow we'd thought ridicule was a thing of the past. Instead, it had become so ordinary that she closed her tormentors out of her consciousness much the way she did buzzing flies.

Who *were* those creeps anyway?

"Hey you. Get back to work," scolded a white haired woman in a slack suit. It had to be Belle, because the two miscreants immediately picked up their duties. She appeared to have seen only that they were loafing.

As she strode through the work area, Edward caught up with her and pointed toward us. She smiled in our direction and moved to the counter. Matt and I walked over and introduced ourselves.

With her creamy complexion and pleasant expression, Belle looked like she should have been arranging roses in a florist shop rather than riding herd on a night crew. But the tone of her voice and her air of quiet efficiency made it clear that she was in charge.

"Nicole is a valuable employee," she immediately informed us, as she monitored the two young men. "Unlike the others, she hustles the whole time she's here. She's pretty messy. She soaks herself when she washes dishes—I'm still working with her on that. And she's slow. But she can do the work of three employees."

She pointed toward a sponge, and the thin youth handed it to her. "She'll be the first to be laid off, though, because she can't 'work counter,' " she said, as she wiped off the mustard dispenser. "I'm training her to use the cash register, but it's slow going. She's afraid. She's worked counter a few times, and the customers have said some terrible things to her. To Edward, too."

"Like what?"

"I'm not going to say." She removed the lid, and handed the dispenser to the young man to refill.

I wanted to grab Nicole and Edward and whisk them away at top speed. But where else would they find work?

"Belle," I asked cautiously, "Nicole has mentioned a Connie and Juan who work here. Is one of those young men Juan?"

"Oh, no. Connie and Juan are out sick. Those two kids are temporary hires." Her gray-blue eyes met mine. "Why? Did you see what they were doing just now?"

So she *had* seen it. "Well, yes. . . . "

"They're leaving as soon as Connie and Juan return. I can't have that kind of nonsense in my shop."

Matt and I glanced at each other in silent relief. At

She had to deal w/ being tormented

least the harassment was usually confined to the customers.

"We appreciate what you're doing for Nicole and Edward," I said. Matt seconded my sentiment.

"Well, some kids need more help than others. I try to do what I can." A man buying a bowl of chowder was becoming impatient with Edward, and Belle left to straighten out the problem.

Matt and I began our walk home. No discussion was needed. We both knew Belle had joined the crowd of Nicole's—and Edward's—protective saints.

That November, the night before Thanksgiving, Nicole and Edward proved they could give to Belle as well as receive. Perhaps they did so on other occasions, but this was one time I found out about it.

"Hi. Aunt Vicky's dinner will be on the table in an hour," I said cheerily, when I called her at noon on Thanksgiving day to wake her. I'd agreed the day before to be her alarm clock for the turkey dinner.

"We can't go," Nicole mumbled. "We didn't get to bed until 7:00 this morning."

"Seven! How come?"

Nicole's account was confusing, but I pieced together that Belle had dismissed the entire crew at 2:00 A.M. When Nicole and Edward realized that Belle intended to remain alone to clean and 'close,' they refused to leave.

"It's not safe for you to be here by yourself," they had told her, and they had stayed until 6:00 A.M. to help her finish the job.

Nicole was angry, though, because she and Edward would miss Thanksgiving completely. They were too tired to attend her aunt's dinner, and they couldn't go to

Edward's family gathering in the evening because they had to be back at work by 6:00 P.M.

"I'm sorry," I commiserated. "Would you like me to bring you some dinner around five o'clock? It's the least I can do."

"Whatever. . . . " Right then all she wanted to do was sleep.

At 5:00 P.M., I arrived at the apartment with two plates of food. Nicole let me in. Her hair was still wet from being washed, but she was already in her uniform. Edward was padding around in his trousers and T-shirt.

"Is Shelley with her father?" I called, as I put the plates in the oven.

"No. He took his girlfriend, and they went to Palm Springs. Shelley got invited over to her boyfriend's house."

I walked into the living room. "Me and Edward gotta keep getting ready to go to work, okay?" Nicole said from the bedroom.

"Certainly. Don't mind me." I settled into the couch.

"Where's my comb?" I heard Edward ask her.

"You've putten it right there, hon." Nicole's response was impatient yet amused.

She appeared in the living room with her purse and a sweater, and deposited them on a wicker chair.

"Did you lock the back door?" she asked him, as she walked into the bathroom.

"Yeah."

She emerged from the bathroom, tucked a tube of hand cream and a wad of Kleenex in her purse, and stood for a moment thinking. Then she returned to the bedroom and brought out her phosphorescent orange jacket and her crash helmet. These were placed on the chair.

Well, I'll be darned, I thought to myself. *She's planning ahead.*

"I guess we can eat now," she said, pulling her hair into its twist and pinning it.

I hopped up, got the plates, and placed them on the table. Eating took a little longer than expected, because the two diners were so playful—Nicole kept spearing Edward's food, and he retaliated by tickling her—but eventually they finished, and we gathered at the door to leave.

"Aren't you going to turn off the lights?" I asked, as Nicole turned to gaze at the living room. The amber glass lamps were on at a low wattage.

"No. I always leave them on when we go to work. It looks so pretty when we come back."

Edward was the last one out. He locked the door, and we all went down the steps. Within minutes they were on their way to The Chowder Bowl, she astride the moped and he on her old bike.

It looks like the work ethic is taking hold after all, I thought, as I got in my car and began the drive home. Maybe I was wrong eight months ago when I forecast her future. Perhaps she *will* move to Fremont one day, but her life will be different from what I'd pictured then. After all, she can't get SSI. She's apparently unable to have children. She hardly has time for friends anymore.

Yet, in spite of the problems and disappointments—or because of them—she was adjusting, learning, growing. She seemed to be happier. So did Edward. As evidence, the accidents and illnesses were diminishing.

I just hoped she could keep her job.

Christmas morning she was still chipper. Why, I

don't know. As on Thanksgiving, she and Edward had worked the night before. Even so, for some reason she was in rare form.

The day before, she'd told us to go ahead with the present unwrapping; she and Edward would get there when they could rouse themselves. We had done so, and were sitting, glassy-eyed, in a sea of torn wrapping papers, ribbons, and boxes when Nicole hustled in the door trailed by Edward.

She plopped a tiny brown and white wind-up dog on the floor. It toddled along, sat down, barked, and repeated the sequence until it fell over.

"That's my dog," she announced. Edward had given it to her in lieu of the real dog Charlotte had forbidden in the apartment. The creature was so absurd we couldn't help but laugh.

It was all the encouragement Nicole needed. Throwing herself into the mess of papers, she festooned herself with loops of ribbons. They went over her ears, around her head at nose level, and a few hung off her glasses. Edward was convulsed. I began to worry.

"Hey, Nicole," asked her amused brother, who was lounging on the couch. "What do you think you're getting for Christmas?"

"I already know. It's sitting in the garage," she said, deadpan. Everyone roared. "She's going to get the keys," she added, when I got up to get more coffee. We laughed even harder.

"Here," squeaked Jill, thrusting a gift at her. "Open this. It's from Mom."

Nicole inspected it. I'd wrapped the object "paper bag style" so that tissue folds flared above where the ribbon had been tied. She peered down the recesses of the folds like a woodpecker surveying a knothole.

"What in the hell has she done now?" she muttered, as she began tearing at the tissue. When at last she pulled out a steamer rack—a perforated metallic contraption with collapsing sides—she set it down on the floor and solemnly studied it.

"I knew she'd do something weird," she commented.

The entire family lost the last semblance of its dignity. We howled and slapped the floor like fools.

It was too much for Nicole. Whooping her high cackle, she began clapping her hands and banging her feet on the floor. Within thirty seconds her flushed face had contorted into a grimace, and her body was shaking with silent spasms.

The family's laughter stopped abruptly. I laid my hand on her shoulder. "Okay, okay . . . " I said soothingly.

"Whooooooo whoooooooo whoooooo," she whimpered, trying to quiet down. The spasms erupted again and again, but gradually she gained control. The last time she had been that hysterical had been at Disneyland. Now all she needed were calming words.

That, too, was growth.

It was growth for me, too. The fact that I had remained composed was evidence of how far I had come.

After she'd rested against the couch for a minute or two, she and Edward unwrapped the rest of their presents. When the last one had been opened, Edward took charge of handing out their presents to us. David and Jill each received a five dollar book of coupons to The Chowder Bowl. Matt and I were given a shoe box wrapped in Christmas paper.

"It's all we can afford," Edward said, shyly.

I pulled the paper off. The box was empty except for a hand-lettered sign on the bottom: "ALL OUR LOVE."

Matt and I hugged them both and pinned it up on

the bulletin board.

They ate some brunch with us, and then left for home to get more sleep before having to go to work at 6:00 P.M.

9

*Do you know how
I could prove
I'm handicapped?*

Nicole was kept on at The Chowder Bowl through the holidays, but when the crowds dwindled in January, Belle put her back on a call-in basis. Her phone call rate to me adjusted accordingly. At times I felt as if a phone receiver were permanently attached to my ear.

Her topics at this point were money problems and Old Faithful—her need to borrow the camper *now.*

"Can't I please use it? Just this once? I'll never ask for it again."

That was as likely as my growing antlers. But one day I was so exhausted that I was ready to do anything to get her off the phone—even allow her to set a precedent.

"Yes," I sighed. "You may use it."

She was at our house in record time. I handed her the key, and retreated upstairs to my bed. Five minutes later I could still hear the motor running as she adjusted the seat and mirrors.

"See, sweet Mommy? There wasn't any need to

worry, was there?" she said, when she returned four hours later, the camper and she both intact.

The precedent set, she increased the pressure. She also informed us that her father's plan for a car, when and if she moved to Lemon Grove, was too indefinite. She was going to buy one right away, and she marched to the bank to get a loan. The loan officer informed her it would have to be co-signed.

"You wouldn't co-sign a loan, would you?" she asked her father, then me.

"No."

She asked both Gordon Wade and her Rehab counselor if they would co-sign it, and was told no.

That left her with only one option: her parents would have to be persuaded to lend her the money.

She set to work immediately. "Hi, Mom," she chirruped over the phone. "Me and Edward have decided to let Daddy buy us a car, and then each year we'll give him our income tax refund until it's paid off."

That ploy not working, she tried a different one the next day.

"Hi, Mom. Me and Edward got soaked in the rain last night riding to work. We were shivering and cold. That's not healthy."

"Maybe you should buy ponchos."

"I don't need a poncho! I need a car!" she shouted.

I was sympathetic, but I saw no solution to their predicament. "You can't pay us back that kind of money, Nicole. Why, with you working such short hours, you can't even afford the gas and upkeep on a car."

"I got so many problems," she wailed. "We need a car and can't afford one. We got all these bills. The clinic says Edward can't see his doctor anymore. . . . "

"Hold on. Would you like me to look at the bills

and explain them to you?"

"Whatever. . . . " She really *was* distressed, if she was going to let me look at their medical statements.

"When should I come?"

"Me and Edward will be back from the laundromat about five."

At 5:15 I pulled up to their apartment. No one was home. I leaned against the car and waited.

In a few minutes Nicole came putt-putting around the corner, laundry in pillowcases stuffed into the wire baskets on either side of the rear wheel, a large box of detergent strapped precariously behind the seat. What looked like a sock bounced out of one of the cases as the moped hit a small pothole.

"I have only two more trips," she shouted from under her helmet. The detergent fell off the rack.

Edward pedaled into view, stretching his neck over a bag of laundry tied in front of his handlebars. He stopped and retrieved the sock.

I was appalled. "Is this the way you do the laundry all the time?" Of course, it had to be. No bus went from their apartment to the shopping center.

"Yes . . . no . . . ," Nicole said, as she picked up the detergent. "Sometimes I tie the hamper onto the moped, so I can do it all in one trip, but it usually falls off before I get there."

I couldn't imagine how she could balance their huge hamper on the moped, even with ropes.

"Would you watch our bikes a minute?" she asked.

"Sure."

She and Edward carried their pillowcases up the stairs and into the apartment, while I imagined what doing their laundry must be like when it rained.

"Edward says he'll ride over and get the rest of the stuff," Nicole called down, when she reappeared on the landing. "You can come on up."

"Do you carry groceries home the same way?" I asked, as I mounted the stairs.

"Yeah."

"Don't things get broken?"

Suddenly recognizing that my concern could be exploited, she planted her fists on her hips and blocked my passage. "You want to see the pieces of the salad oil bottle?" she demanded, her face next to mine. "It leaked onto everything in the bag. You didn't know I needed a car that bad. You didn't know that, did you? *Did you?*"

The defiance in her eyes would have shrunk an M-1 tank to toy size.

"DID you!"

"No, Nicole," I mumbled. Triumphant, she let me pass.

"Okay, where are the bills?" I asked, changing the subject as quickly as possible.

She dumped their "file" drawer upside down on the dining table, and I began sorting through the contents. After fifteen minutes or so, I sat back in my chair.

"We're doing real good, aren't we?"

"Not exactly," I said. "The reason the clinic refused to let Edward see his doctor is that his bill—which is now $475—has been sent to a collection agency."

"Why?" she exclaimed.

"Because Edward made only two of those fifty-dollar payments."

Her face crinkled in confusion. "What fifty-dollar payments?"

I tried to jog her memory. She recalled having been to the clinic, but couldn't remember the outcome. At least she said she couldn't.

As that was history anyway, I returned to outlining their debts. "You, too, have a bill at the collection agency. Remember when you had the infection lanced under your arm?"

"Yeah . . . ?"

"Apparently you've paid nothing on it. The total comes to $108."

She stalked out of the room. I continued talking, more to myself than her. "Medi-Cal will pay fifty-eight dollars of it, as soon as you send them a receipt from the collection agency for fifty dollars, your pay stubs for the last two months, these forms I have in my hand, and a statement of your distance to and from work."

My God. This paperwork is unbelievable.

"Would you like your father or me to . . . ?" I called into the bedroom.

The predicted answer shot right back: "No." She returned to the living room with the laundry and sat down on the couch to fold it.

"In five minutes 'Little House on the Prairie' begins," she said with a forced cheeriness that signaled an end to the financial discussion.

When are you going to allow us to help you manage your money and insurance, I asked her silently, as I watched her fold towels.

"Well, I've got to go," I said out loud. "It's getting late."

"Thanks for coming over, Mom," Nicole said, as she turned on the television.

When I arrived home, I found Matt heating up leftovers.

"I thought I was going to be eating alone," he said. "Jill's having pizza with friends, and I was sure you'd forgotten where you lived."

I gave him a kiss of reassurance, tied an apron around his waist, and proceeded to talk non-stop about Nicole's and Edward's transportation and medical bill problems.

While we ate, we discussed their situation. By the time we were through, we'd arrived at some decisions.

One was that we'd buy Nicole a car.

"We've written in our wills that she'll have money when we die," I'd argued. "Why not help her while we're still alive? A car would make her life so much easier."

Matt agreed. He'd been thinking along those same lines during the past few months. "The cost of a car is only a fraction of what we would've spent on her college education."

The other decision was that their bills would have to be paid off before the car purchase would occur.

"But Matt, that's impossible. They've made it clear they can't manage their money."

"You don't understand," he said, his eyes shining impishly. "If she wants the car, she has to let me take over the bill-paying."

I grinned. "How can she refuse?"

She didn't, when we presented the package to her the following Tuesday. She conferred with a pop-eyed Edward for two seconds and then agreed.

"But it has to be a loan," she insisted. They had their pride.

"Call it a loan then."

She gave a little bounce on the sofa. "When can we go look at cars? I know where there's a Toyota lot that has a . . . "

"Hey, slow down there, young lady. Every week you will deliver to me twenty-five dollars. When the debts are paid, I'll let you know. That'll be at least six months from now. Then we'll look at cars."

"Oh. . . . "

"Now I'm going upstairs," Matt said, easing himself out of his armchair. "I have some work to do." He picked up his briefcase and headed for his office.

"You can turn on the tv, if you want," I said, getting up myself. "I've got to put away the food."

Edward put his arm around Nicole and whispered something to her. "Edward's chosed the date," she said to me. The tone was matter-of-fact.

"What date?"

"For our wedding."

"November first," Edward said. "That's the first date Belle can give me two weeks off."

Was he serious?

"It's only going to be me and Edward and our families," Nicole said.

"We can't afford anything more than that," Edward added, his arm still around Nicole.

"Edward, the bride's parents pay for the wedding. You can have as big a wedding as you want."

"I keep telling you that," Nicole said to him.

Edward studied me through his dusky lenses. He withdrew his arm and looked at her. "You mean she could wear a long white dress and a veil and carry flowers?"

"Yes."

His eyes moistened. "She'd look so cute. Could Jill sing? And lots of people come?"

"Not lots of people!" exclaimed Nicole. "I'd be too scared!"

Edward's face fell.

"I *would*. I couldn't stand up in front of a lot of people."

"Well, you decide between you," I interrupted, "and then let me know. I'll be happy to help you plan any kind of wedding you want."

I walked into the kitchen. They discussed it some

more, and then Edward turned on the television. It was time for his show.

Well. What a change. Now it was Edward who was bringing up the subject, and Nicole who was balking.

Nothing further was said about a wedding during the next six months, but Edward and Nicole brought Matt their drawer of papers, and they placed twenty-five dollars in his hand each week.

·   Sometimes they did, that is. Matt went empty-handed for a few weeks while their television set, the one salvaged from a neighbor's trash, acquired a new picture tube. (Some of their income tax refund went toward that as well.)

As soon as the weather began to warm up, Nicole was put back on full-time status at The Chowder Bowl, and the payments began coming in regularly. Raises—fifteen cents an hour for Nicole and twenty-five for Edward—helped. Some weeks they brought Matt double the agreed-upon amount.

In July the debt was retired. True to his word, Matt took them to look at cars. They wandered in and out of used car lots, Matt asking questions of the salesmen, Nicole and Edward tagging silently along.

"Are you making a decision, Daddy?" Nicole asked him whenever he talked at length with a salesperson. She hoped he'd find a Toyota Corolla, preferably white, but she was remaining flexible.

"Not yet," Matt kept saying.

At last he settled on a red Datsun, nine years old. It cost more than he'd intended to spend, but he wanted a car that got good gas mileage.

Nicole was handed the keys. "Try driving it," Matt said, letting Edward in the back before he took the passenger seat.

She approached the task as if the entire California

Highway Patrol was lined up ready to cite her. After adjusting everything within reach and instructing her passengers to fasten their seatbelts, she checked for moving cars in front of her, behind her, and on either side of her in the sales lot. Then she turned on the motor, released the brake, and shifted into "Drive." The car gave a little leap forward.

"Easy now," Matt cautioned.

"Yes, Daddy." She eased the car out of the lot and into the street. During the drive around the block, she maintained her vigilance; any moving vehicle within 200 feet was given the right-of-way.

"You like it?" Matt asked her, after she brought the Datsun back to its original parking space.

"It's okay," she said, smiling her Mona Lisa smile.

Matt completed the paperwork while Nicole and Edward examined the details of their new possession. When Matt was done, he drove the car to our house. "You will not drive it until you're covered by insurance," he said.

The postponement was almost more than she could bear. Sunday, she arrived at our house to vacuum the interior. Monday, she and Edward washed the exterior. She also tied a tiny knitted mouse onto the rearview mirror where it dangled daintily over the dashboard.

"You can take it home now," Matt said on Tuesday, handing her the keys. "The insurance company just called to say you're covered."

She opened the door and slid into the driver's seat. "We're going to bring you money every week for the insurance and to pay you back for the car," she promised.

"Okay, Nicole, you do that."

"By the way, where are you going to park at work?" I asked, bending to look in her window. "Isn't parking down there expensive?"

"Yes, but I'm applying for a handicapped permit."

I exchanged quizzical looks with Matt. "How did you think to do that?"

"There's all those parking spaces with those, like, you know, little signs on them. I asked the man in the little booth who they were for, and he said 'the handicapped,' so I asked him how much they costed, and he said 'They're free.' So I said I was handicapped, and I wanted one." She pondered a second or two. "Do you know how I could prove I'm handicapped?"

It took a minute before I could close my jaw. "I'm sure you'll think of something," I said, laughing. "Like you said, you may be retarded, but you're not stupid."

She looked at me in confusion, and then broke into a grin. "Yeah. . . . "

She casually placed her elbow on the window frame, gave a quick glance through the rearview mirror, and drove off.

"I hope we're doing the right thing," Matt muttered, as we watched her turn the corner.

We waited each day after that for a phone call from the California Highway Patrol or a hospital reporting that she'd been killed. As the weeks passed and none came, our anxiety diminished. Finally it reached the point where we worried about her driving no more than we did about that of our other two children.

Meanwhile, she was denied a free parking permit at work. (She tried using her handicapped bus pass as proof of her status, but the man in the little booth was unimpressed.) That was only a minor flaw in the larger picture, however. Every week on one of their days off, she and Edward and their friends took to the highways. They went horseback riding in Griffeth Park, picnicked at Descanso Gardens, revisited Disneyland, inspected the sights in Hollywood, and camped in the mountains.

"How do you find all these places?" I asked.

"Edward reads the map and tells me where to go."

Why hadn't I thought of that? She rarely drove without him in the car with her. I stopped worrying about her inability to read street signs.

The excursions began to dwindle toward the end of August. Edward had definitely decided that he was tired of bachelorhood, and their free time was used to prepare for a November first wedding.

"Why do you suppose he's become so enthusiastic about getting married?" Matt asked me.

"I haven't a clue. Whatever was bothering him in the past must have been resolved."

Edward was not only ready, he had clear ideas, and he expressed them. "I want it held outdoors," he said. As he described what he had in mind, I realized that his inspiration was a wedding we had all attended the previous May in an exquisitely manicured rose garden.

"Well, our patio is too small, but maybe we could use Charlotte's yard." Hardly a rose garden, it was more a cactus-succulent-and-wind-chime experience.

He conferred with Nicole. "That'd be okay." We called Charlotte, who was delighted. The place was set.

The weather, however, wasn't. "If it's rainy or cold, we'll move indoors," I decided. "Charlotte's house can hold twenty or thirty people."

"Twenty or thirty!" Nicole gasped. "I wanted just family."

"That *is* just family. If you add up all your cousins, their husbands, and Edward's family, that's twenty-six people—not including children."

"No," she whimpered. "I'll say my vows in the house and then come out."

Edward took her hand. "Aw, you can't do that, Nicole," he pleaded. "We have to do it right. All those people have to come, and we have to invite our friends, too . . ."

"No. No." Her eyes filled with tears.

I broke in. "Look. Let's forget about the guest list for now. Nicole, why don't you and I have some fun? We'll look at wedding dress patterns, cakes in bakeries, and wedding invitations. Decisions on those things have to be made."

Edward patted her hand.

"Well, okay . . . ," she sniffled.

As much as Edward, I wanted her to look forward to sharing her wedding with family and friends. The bridal activities would do the trick—I hoped.

We began them on her next day off. Her Aunt Vicky was a seamstress, and she conferred with Nicole and Shelley and me in the fabric store.

"You'll have to make your entrance down those five steps at the back of Charlotte's house, so you'd better forget about a veil over your face and a floor-length dress," Vicky suggested to Nicole. "You don't want to fall."

Nicole took the news indifferently. Anything Vicky advised, Nicole accepted. So did Shelley, when it came time to discuss the maid-of-honor dress. Finally, Vicky and I made the decisions about both the women's dresses.

Yet the project had piqued Nicole's interest a little. As we left the shop, she said, "I guess I'll have to buy a lacy slip and white shoes, won't I?"

"Yes, I guess you will."

Our next excursion was to the bakery. And there was Nicole's Achilles' heel. She scanned the photograph album of wedding cakes and looked at the bridal couple ornaments lined up on the shelf, and she began asking questions.

A rosy cheeked saleswoman in a white uniform answered them. Yes, the cake could be pink and white. No, the bakery had never had a cake fall apart as it was carried out the door. Why? Because the tiers were delivered in separate boxes and assembled at the reception. No, the cake didn't have to be white inside; the bakery offered many types.

We left the shop with Nicole carrying a box of cake slices. That evening she conducted a cake sampling session with Edward.

Nicole's enthusiasm for her wedding was growing. When she selected her wedding invitations, she suggested we order fifty of them.

"Are you sure?" I asked.

"Yeah. Then we can invite all our friends."

My selling job had gone so well, I felt a momentary twinge of guilt.

Over the next few weeks she and Edward addressed the invitations (Edward and Shelley actually did them —Nicole, exhausted from cooking everyone dinner, fell asleep on our couch), had conferences with the minister, selected their rings, chose the music for the processional, and Edward went to the dentist.

"Edward went where?"

"To the dentist," Nicole said. "One tooth got taken out last week. Tomorrow he's going to get two more pulled."

I looked at Edward. His gaze fled to the floor.

"The first time he insisted I hold his hand, but now he tells me to go away," Nicole bragged.

"How many cavities?" I asked, finding my voice.

"Five," Nicole answered. "They'll all be filled before the wedding."

"Whatever possessed you to go?" I asked Edward.

He grinned sheepishly. "I got a toothache so bad I couldn't sleep. . . . "

Edward suffered after the next two extractions, because one hole became infected. Penicillin worked its magic, however, and the following week he began having his cavities filled.

At least I assume he did. I was too preoccupied with the mushrooming guest list to ask.

"Really? How wonderful," old friends were saying, when I ran into them and told them Nicole was getting married. Their interest seemed so genuine, I'd invite them. I hoped they'd come, but if it rained, we were headed for disaster. Charlotte's house could hold thirty people at the most.

Each time I told Nicole about someone else who might be coming, it fed her mounting excitement. By the time of the wedding rehearsal, she was so electrified she could have powered every appliance in Charlotte's house. Not even David, who'd arrived the night before, could calm her down.

Bart, the minister, did his best to work around her. He told David, who had assumed charge of the stereo, to start the music for the processional, and directed the rest of us to file through the open glass doors, down the curving brick steps, and through the grass to a tree. Everyone did as instructed. At the tree, we turned to wait for Nicole. She remained on the top step whooping and executing a hula.

"All right, let's try it again," Bart said to the rest of us, recognizing that Nicole had no intention of taking her father's arm and following us. "This time walk slower."

"Here! I'm gonna go first," Nicole giggled, pushing ahead of everyone. Matt took her firmly by the hand and led her to the rear of the line. Bart gave the signal, and

David started the music. This time, everyone paraded more decorously.

Except Nicole. She chose to make her entrance backward and cackling.

"Matt, what is she going to do tomorrow?" I groaned, as her laughter resounded through the garden.

After Bart directed us once through the recessional, we called it quits. Mary Brichant and I conferred for the final time about our dresses, and Matt and I were introduced to the darkly handsome Juan, Edward's best man. Then we all scattered, each of us to attend to last minute preparations for the next day.

We woke the morning of the wedding with sun coming in the window. Matt and I sighed with relief. David left to pick up Shelley and Nicole, and I sat down to weave a garland of flowers for Nicole's hair.

"I'm headed over there to set up the chairs," Matt said. "Kind of warm, isn't it?"

I wiped perspiration off my nose. "Yes, it is. What time is it?"

"Just past 9:30."

I'm this sticky, and it's only 9:30? I stepped outside. The sky was a deep ultramarine unmarred by a single cloud.

"Matt!" I wailed. "It's going to be a scorcher. I *knew* I hadn't thought of everything. The guests are going to fry. The cake is going to melt. The drinks are going to be warm . . . "

"Calm down," he ordered. "I'll pick up some ice at Safeway on the way over there."

"I'm coming, too."

We picked up the ice, and raced to Charlotte's. Vicky's husband's truck was in the driveway. "What's going on?" Matt and I asked each other, as we hurried through the house.

We were greeted by a virtual Fairyland in the garden. Pink and white flowers graced linen-covered serving tables. The white folding chairs were set up in rows with bows of white satin lining the aisle that led to the tree. Tall baskets of flowers banked an archway where Edward and Nicole would say their vows.

The elves were still at work—Vicky and her daughters unloading more flowers from the truck, her husband packing the bottles of sparkling cider in lined trashcans full of ice, and Charlotte arranging the cake layers, which had just been delivered, in her refrigerator.

"This is beautiful!" I exclaimed, applauding.

"How long have you been here?" Matt asked, grinning with delight.

"Since six," Vicky said. "We've done a lot of weddings in our family, and we saw you needed help, so we all pitched in."

Maybe the guests would swelter, but I couldn't imagine a prettier setting in which to do it.

I wanted to help, but the arrival of Edward and Juan in their navy blue suits and boutonnieres reminded me that time was passing. I flew home to see how Nicole was doing.

Dressed in her slip, nylons, and new shoes, she was sitting on the toilet seat playing "keep-away" with Jill's hairbrush. Only when Jill got angry did Nicole hand it over so that her sister could arrange her hair and place the wreath of flowers above it.

"You look real pretty," Shelley said, when Jill zipped Nicole into her wedding gown. I agreed. The wreath and the simple white satin dress were transforming her into a lovely bride.

"It's 11:35," Matt called to me, bounding past Jill and Shelley going downstairs. "I'll be ready in five minutes."

"Wait until you see Grandma Charlotte's yard," I bubbled to Nicole, as I put my dress on. "Flowers all over everywhere, and ribbon on the chairs, and an archway. . . . "

I'd said the wrong thing. Nicole grew quiet, her eyebrows assuming the inverted distress "V" as her stage fright returned.

"Momma," she said grabbing my hands and squeezing them too tightly, "I woke up this morning and thought about all the people that are going to be there, and I lay there and cried. I was so scared. . . . "

"Come now," I said, "you haven't even seen your bouquet. Let's go downstairs and get it."

As I led her down the hall, Bartok, our sheltie, came trotting up the stairs.

"Hi, Bartoky-Poo!" Nicole crowed. Galvanized by her greeting, he leaped ecstatically toward her face, his paws sliding down her dress.

"Nicole!" I shrieked. I sent Bartok packing, and frantically searched her dress for paw marks. There were none, amazingly.

She burst into laughter and sailed down the stairs. I staggered after her.

While Matt and David alternately complimented Nicole on how pretty she looked and calmed her down, I retrieved the bouquets from the refrigerator, and handed them to the three women.

"What's this? Spaghetti?" Nicole chortled, when she saw that hers had long ribbons trailing from it.

We drove her to Charlotte's and ushered her into a back bedroom. It was a quarter to one. As I helped Charlotte with last minute details, I looked out through the glass doors. Every seat was taken in the garden.

"Grandma!" Jill suddenly bellowed from the back

bedroom. "Have you got any nail polish remover?"

Charlotte dropped the sugar tongs and scooted into her bathroom to look, while Vicky and I ran into the back bedroom. Nicole was sitting on the floor painting her nails, the bottle of blood red nail polish resting on the folds of her white dress.

I grabbed the bottle. Jill seized Nicole's hand and began scouring the scarlet nails with polish remover. Vicky searched her dress for spills. Again, amazingly, nothing. One of the cousins snapped pictures, and David and Matt poked their heads in to see what was going on. Nicole found the pandemonium hilarious.

Returning to the family room, we found that Mary had arrived with Edward's two brothers and his sister. She introduced us to them—we had never met before—and I pinned a corsage on Mary.

"It's one o'clock, and everyone's here, so I guess we can begin," Bart said to the gathering. We all took a deep breath and began to line up. Matt went down the hall to get Nicole, and Jill stepped out on the top step to sing the song she'd chosen for her sister's wedding. Her voice floated sweetly above the tape recording of my piano accompaniment.

> "Is it really me?
> Is it really true?
> Suddenly I'm beautiful
> Being here with you . . . "

Nicole appeared in the family room on her father's arm, took one look through the glass doors at the sea of people, and her ebullience turned to terror.

"No, Daddy, no, no," she cried, huddling against him, her eyes filling with tears.

"Hey, sweetheart," Matt said soothingly. "Don't be afraid. All those people out there are your friends. . . . "

"Moments ago
I was alone
Hoping that this could be.
Now here I am
Safe in your arms
And I'm no longer lonely . . . "

"No, No, No," Nicole insisted. "I can't. . . . " Her
face was blotched from crying.

"Hey there now," Matt said, his arm around her.
"You're supposed to be happy! This is your wedding
day!"

"Is it really me?
Is it really true?
Suddenly I'm beautiful
All because of you."

Jill stepped back into the house, and took her place
in line. David started "Endless Love," the music that
Nicole and Edward had selected for the processional,
and we began filing out the door.

Bart went first. He was followed by an elegant Juan,
and then a self-conscious Edward. The latter walked
with his eyes down, his arms held rigidly in front of
him, one hand gripping the knuckles of the other.
Shelley paraded down the steps holding her bouquet
aloft like the Statue of Liberty's flame. Jill, Mary
Brichant, Charlotte, and I succeeded her, one by one,
until all of us had reached our assigned positions by the
tree. Turning, we waited for the entrance of the bride.

She appeared in the doorway, her father quite literally holding her up. His right arm was around her waist,
his left hand supporting her left arm.

Clutching her bouquet like it was a lifeline thrown
a sinking swimmer, she wobbled forward one step. Matt
bent his head and whispered words of encouragement.

She took another step. And, falteringly, another.

I watched her awkward progress, saw her contorted, tear-stained face, and mourned. Why couldn't she have been serene and beautiful for this one moment? Edward must be so embarrassed.

I turned to glance at him. His eyes were on her, but his face was radiant. I realized that he was seeing something entirely different. Coming toward him was the woman he loved, and he had never seen her look more beautiful. She didn't have a veil, and her gown didn't sweep the ground, but those things were unimportant. She was an enchanted vision in white. Roses crowned her head, and satin ribbons danced from the flowers in her hands.

Tears stung my eyes. *Oh God, how absolutely terrific. How fortunate she is. How fortunate we all are to have this young man.*

Matt, his arm around Nicole, his hand still supporting her elbow, delivered her to Edward. "Endless Love" faded out, but Matt remained beside her for a minute to make certain she was steady on her feet. Then he sat down next to me.

Bart spoke privately with her, soothing her, as Edward watched sympathetically. Finally her trembling diminished enough that Bart felt he could begin.

"Friends and family," he said in a resonant voice, "we have come here today to celebrate the union of Edward and Nicole." Addressing the young couple, he read from the *Bible* and *The Prophet* advising them on how to conduct their married lives.

The longer he talked, the more Nicole relaxed. His words meant nothing to her, so she began peeking over her shoulder to see who was in the audience. Spotting Penny and Francisco, she gave them a little wave.

"Nicole," Bart said, bringing her attention back to

the business at hand, "I'm going to read you a description of Edward and ask you if it describes him." Nicole waited dutifully. "Edward, child of the beach, lover of rock and roll music, watcher of movies—especially of films on the martial arts—liker of people, television, and baseball. Edward is a man who is not afraid to work. He is Nicole's eyes, her lover, her 'precious.' Easily upset, yet easy to forgive. He is a man who lives and sees life simply, who sees his life only with Nicole.

"Nicole, is this the Edward you know and love?"

"Yes," she whispered.

Bart turned to Edward. "Edward, I'm going to read a description of Nicole and ask you if it describes her. Nicole—a woman who laughs and giggles at life, who loves to swim and ride horses, when she has time. She is Edward's lover. She likes to go places, especially with Edward. She's proud of learning to live alone, as she says, 'the hard way.' She treasures her freedom, wishing she could stay home more to cook and sew. She is tender and understanding. Edward says, 'She makes me feel so good.'

"Edward, is this the Nicole you know and love?"

"Yes," he said softly.

"Edward, take Nicole's hand and repeat after me." Nicole handed her bouquet to Shelley, and put her right hand in Edward's. Looking steadily at her, Edward repeated that he would love and cherish her as long as he lived.

When it was Nicole's turn to say her vows, she kept her eyes on Bart. He pronounced only one word at a time, but she needed all her powers of concentration to remember them correctly. This was no time for romantic gazing at Edward.

The rings were exchanged. Bart offered a short prayer, and the service was over.

"Edward and Nicole," Bart said, "by the powers invested in me and by the vows you have made today, I now pronounce you husband and wife. Edward, you may kiss the bride."

Nicole turned toward Edward, and he gave her a shy kiss.

Bart turned them both around to face the seated congregation. "Ladies and gentlemen, I take the privilege of presenting to you Edward and Nicole Brichant."

Handel's "Hallelujah Chorus" burst forth from the stereo speakers. David was right on cue. "Hallelujah! Hallelujah! Hallelujah!" rang through the afternoon air as the newlyweds, arm in arm, made their way up the aisle past the clapping guests.

The rest of us followed after them in the order that had been prescribed at the rehearsal.

"Good grief!" I exclaimed, when we were all in the house. "The reception line!"

While everyone yelled suggestions, someone opened the front door and we all flowed out to the driveway. There we made a raggle-taggle formation. It was none too soon, for the guests were trailing right behind us.

Edward wound up first in line. Nicole stood next to him. As each of the well-wishers passed by, he smiled and shook hands, but his wife, free at last to enjoy herself, bubbled with joy. She enthusiastically introduced members of Edward's family to her father, who was standing next to her, and dispensed hugs to the family friends she hadn't seen for years.

Edward's and her friends came through the line, too. Roger, neatly attired in a crisp shirt and slacks. Bill, looking healthier but still too frail. Penny and Francisco, holding hands. Andrea in tears, overcome by the beauty of the occasion. And Dottie with her hand decorously through the arm of Todd. Nicole hugged all of them.

When the receiving line broke up, I was too busy playing hostess to see much of her. But coming and going I caught glimpses of her beside Edward eating her quiche and fresh fruit, chatting with people, cutting the three-tiered cake, and tossing her bouquet. Through it all she looked serene—at last.

The next day they packed our camper for their honeymoon. That night they drove by our house to say good-bye.

"Hi, Mr. and Mrs. Kaufman," Shelley called from the back of the camper.

"Hello, Shelley." Shelley would be with them for two days. Nicole would put her on a plane in Fresno on Wednesday so that she would be back in time for her Thursday morning work schedule at the convalescent home.

"Osamu has rented the trailer, and it's in place and all the utilities are hooked up," Matt told them, as we stood in the alley. "Here's a map, Edward. The directions tell you how to get to Lemon Grove, and once you're there, how to find the orchard where the trailer is. If you have any trouble, here's Osamu's phone number." (Osamu was another of Nicole's protective saints.)

"Okay . . . Dad," Edward said smartly. Below his jeans were new boots, just like the ones Matt wore when he went to the ranches. Matt put his arm around Edward's shoulder and squeezed it. Edward swung up into the passenger seat.

Nicole gave Jill, Matt, and me hugs, and then climbed up behind the steering wheel. I stood by her window.

"Oh, yeah. Thanks for the refrigerator," she said.

"They delivered it today."

"You're welcome, Mrs. Brichant. You're not driving straight through, are you?"

"Oh, no. We'll camp tonight at that place where we camped once before—you know, by the stream."

"Good. We'll see you next weekend then."

Nicole started the engine. "Bye, Mom," Edward said, leaning forward to wave at me.

"Good-bye, Son. Good-bye, Nicole—and you, too, Shelley."

Shelley, noticing me poking my head in and saying something to her, removed her Walkman headgear. "What?"

"I said 'good-bye.' "

"Oh. Bye!" She grinned at me, waved, and replaced the headgear.

Seconds later the camper had turned the corner, and they were gone.

"I bet they're bored stiff," Matt said to me as we drove north on Saturday. "There's nothing to do up there. They don't even have television. . . . "

"I know. . . . "

As we pulled into the grove, we found Edward picking pomegranates from a stray bush by the road. He saw us, ran to the trailer, and called Nicole. She appeared at the door wiping her hands on her apron.

"Hi! Come see the trailer!" she called.

We all squeezed into their temporary quarters. It looked as though they'd been living there for years— throw pillows from home on the bed-couch, pot holders dangling from the stove knobs, freshly washed dishes drying in a dish rack, and a small television set on the table.

"Where did you get that?" Matt asked.

"It belongs to Shelley," Edward said. "We can only get one channel, but it has Tic Tac Dough and CHIPS."

Matt and I looked at each other.

"So, do you spend all your time watching tv?" Matt asked Edward.

"Oh, no. Osamu told us where your orange packing houses are," Edward answered, "so we went over, but they weren't running any oranges, so we went to a nut packing house and watched nuts being processed. We tried an olive plant, but it wasn't open. . . . "

"You know those huge rocks down by the corner?" Nicole broke in. "Yesterday we climbed all over them. And we found a lake and went boating the day before that. . . . "

"There's a lake around here?" Matt asked.

"Yeah," Nicole said, "it's down the highway about five miles. And we took Shelley to the Fresno airport."

"Tomorrow we're going horseback riding," Edward said.

"Horseback riding? I've never seen any horses up here."

"They're down the same highway," Nicole said. "And we picked beans for four hours. I told Edward we better see if we could stand it, because if we moved up here, that's the kind of work we'd have to do. And we walk to the turkey farm every night. Hey, I know what let's do! Let's all go see the turkeys!"

She grabbed a sweater and was out the door with Edward behind her before Matt and I could say anything.

"I wonder if we'll ever stop underestimating her," I said, as I took Matt's hand.

He shook his head, wordlessly, and we left the trailer to join them.

A Mother's Epilogue

I sat down at my desk the other afternoon; it was time to stop writing, but to end with Nicole and Edward's wedding was not enough. So much lies ahead, and there were so many thoughts still to be shared. An epilogue seemed in order. I could reflect on the past and write about how a family changes, how brothers and sisters respond, how parents find their way through the school system. Or I could look ahead to concerns we parents face as we grow older. Sorting out my thoughts, I finally decided what seemed most important was to reflect on Nicole's life now—on her being on her own.

But what could I, as mother and researcher—for I am still a member of the Mental Retardation Research Center at the University of California in Los Angeles—say to other parents of mildly retarded young adults who are moving into independence? The obvious came to mind: I would encourage them to be less protective. I would urge them to permit their children to make mistakes, to let them learn through experience, to remain neutral even when they do things that seem unwise.

Although we parents espouse normalization, we often unconsciously undermine it. We postpone taking the steps that will help our children leave the nest. When they finally make the break and are living independently, we judge and control their actions: we make decisions about whom they can see and date; we insist they live in "safe" neighborhoods; we refuse to accept that they are competent enough to make decisions about what foods to eat, or how clean their living quarters should be, or whether they should ride a moped, or drive a car. We reject out of hand such adult activities as drinking, smoking, and watching x-rated movies.

What else should I say in my epilogue? I would reassure parents that even though the early years of independence may be turbulent, as they were with Nicole, they become smoother with the passage of time. Our children may be retarded, but they are not stupid. Experience is a good teacher. They do learn to cope.

Today, five years after her wedding, Matt and I may not hear from Nicole for as long as three weeks. Months go by in which we merely exchange news or relay plans for family occasions. We are serene because we know things are going well for them. She and Edward are busy with their daytime jobs, she cooking hamburgers for a fast-food chain outlet, and he distributing laundry to the floors of a large hotel. Housing and transportation, which have been upgraded to a larger apartment and a newer car, require attention; Nicole keeps the home spotless, and Edward washes the car every weekend. They still are childless, but they borrow Edward's brother's two little boys over the weekends, and return them Sunday nights—a solution which gives the parents respite, and Nicole and Edward the fun of parenting with none of the responsibilities.

Yes, here was the subject matter of my epilogue. The message, upbeat, made a happy finish for the book.

As I mused comfortably on it, my thoughts were interrupted by Nicole appearing in the doorway of my office. I hadn't heard her because she had come up the stairs so quietly.

She stood in the doorway. "Me and Edward, see, we're doing real good. . . ," she began, "we have the rent, see, ok. . . ." The broken sentences continued until she dropped onto the couch and broke into tears. They were tears of humiliation.

They need money, she said. They have a $650 dental bill; originally it was $1,000, but in the past six months they have paid off $350. Both she and Edward need to have their eyeglasses mended, and they can't afford the new parts. Edward has an infected ingrown toenail, and their doctor has referred them to an orthopedist for minor surgery. Meanwhile, because of the pain and swelling, Edward has been home for the past three weeks, so their income has been cut in half. At least he should begin receiving California disability compensation soon. That would help.

"We try so hard, me and Edward," she said, weeping, "but we never seem to get ahead." Touched by her despair, I moved over to the couch and put my arm around her. She cried quietly beside me. Her hands, rough and stained from scouring stubborn restaurant grills, twisted in her lap. I looked at them and thought about how hard she works.

The more I thought about it, the angrier I got. Not at my daughter. At society's indifference to the Nicoles of this country, at its cavalier treatment of mentally retarded individuals who have struggled to become wage earners. Living as they do on the edge of poverty, they have no margin for medical expenses.

What have we done? I asked myself, forgetting about the epilogue. All of us—Nicole's teachers and counselors and Matt and I—have bought the philosophies of normalization and self-reliance. Nicole, in her own pragmatic way, has subscribed to them, too. With all of us working toward those goals, the result is that today Nicole is fully integrated into the community. And what happens? She is penalized. As a member of the working poor, she is deprived of decent health care.

Her place of employment provides no health insurance. Medi-Cal coverage is out of the question, because Edward's and her combined income, though meager, is too high. Coverage would be automatic if she were receiving Supplemental Security Income, but SSI can't be reinstated.

They tried a county hospital once. Nicole drove for 25 minutes to get there, and waited for twelve hours without being seen. Finally she marched up to the desk and began yelling about her sick husband. He was given medical attention. Nicole flatly refused ever to go back there again.

Even so, I saw no other recourse for Edward's upcoming toe surgery. I told her, as I reached for my purse and wrote a check to assuage her creditors at the dental office, that Edward would have to go back to the county hospital. He would just have to sit there and wait until he was seen, even if it took all day. Otherwise, her father and I would have to pay the orthopedist's charge.

"No," she insisted. "It hurts me when you pay our bills." But she took my check, thanked me, and, after giving me a hug, left the house.

I turned back to my desk to pick up my comfortable advice for parents, and realized that Nicole had once again taught me. She had arrived just in time to keep me from writing a facile conclusion, one that suggests that if parents will let go of their mildly retarded children, they will ultimately become self-sufficient members of the community. Maybe I had better rethink what was really happening and what needed saying.

I made myself look objectively at all the ways Matt and I underwrite her independence. We not only give her and Edward money for medical and dental expenses, we also own their apartment (their interest in Lemon Grove gradually dissipated) and rent it to them at only a third of the going rate. We keep them supplied with middle-aged but smoothly running cars. Matt completes their income tax form, and pays anything still due. I help her fill out job application forms (she keeps trying to get a position where she can get benefits and the pay is better than minimum wage, but she is never hired). And Matt and I are available whenever she encounters a problem that she can't solve herself.

Much of our help is economic. Left to their own devices, mentally retarded citizens, whether living on SSI or employed, are poor. They live in lower income housing, and they travel by bus, not car. Most of the informants in our research studies at UCLA are more or less forced to accept these conditions, but, as has been made clear in this book, Nicole is not. Matt and I are able to help, so we provide her with a two-bedroom apartment and a car.

The medical bills and taxes are of a different order. Health care is a necessity. Nicole and Edward can afford occasional doctor visits, but that is all. Knowing this, they often postpone seeing their doctor when something needs attention. Prescriptions remain unpurchased for the same reason. When Matt and I know about it, we make certain they see the doctor, and we pay the bill. I insisted that Edward go to a county hospital for his toe surgery because, being unable to work, he had the time to drive the distance (Edward has a driver's license now, too) and wait all day. If he were working, the lost day's pay would almost equal the cost of a doctor visit. Fortunately Matt and I can afford to underwrite their private medical care. Everytime I write a check, I think about the medically needy retarded wage earners who don't have well-to-do parents.

Nicole and Edward's tax situation is cruelly unjust. Last year they paid $1,042 in taxes to the federal government. (A more benevolent California tax board gave them a "low income credit" as well as a "renters' credit," so they paid no state tax.) They contributed another $1,066 for Social Security, and $134 for State Disability Insurance. The total came to $2,200, or 15% of their taxable income. Talk of irony. If we had all played our cards a little differently and rejected the idea of self-reliance, Nicole could have been *collecting* instead of *supplying* federal funds.

In addition to providing an economic lifeline, Matt and I help Nicole in another vital way. We provide social and emotional support: we are *there*, if and when she and Edward need us. Mentally retarded persons tend to lead highly unstable lives; stressful events easily overwhelm them unless they have someone to whom they can turn. Regional Center counselors can advise, and even intervene when a situation calls for it, but no matter how dedicated professionals are, they can never substitute for a concerned parent or sibling. I once asked a Regional Center supervisor what she would most like to change regarding the quality of life for her clients, and she answered "the rejection by families." Legislative changes, while important to her, were secondary to the need for family support.

Then what should I say to parents in the epilogue? Should I abandon my original idea, and instead advise

them to think carefully before encouraging employment, because as soon as their child has held a job for a
specified length of time, he or she will lose SSI[1] and
Medi-Cal, and the Internal Revenue Service will absorb
an unconscionable part of his or her scanty wages?
Should I warn them that independence for their child
will remain qualified, that their child will continue to
need someone who cares, preferably a family member?

And what about pregnancy? How can I advise parents to remain neutral when they face that issue? And
AIDS, which wasn't even in existence when Nicole entered independence: how can parents be encouraged to
let their children make mistakes, when AIDS is capable
of turning a sexual encounter into a death sentence?

When I began writing, I was confident that I knew
what to say. Now my mind was in total confusion.

It was late afternoon. I went to make supper, but
throughout the evening I tried to sort out my thoughts.
By morning, I was still perplexed about what my message to parents was going to be.

Nicole called just as I returned to my desk.

"Guess what. You'll be so proud of me," she said.
Smugness fairly oozed out of the phone receiver. "Edward got his toe operated on last night, and it didn't cost
us a cent."

"He did? Where did he go?"

"To Emergency at XYZ University Hospital. It's
'betterly' organized than the county hospital. He was
seen right away, and we were all done in three hours."

"How did you learn about it?"

"Oh, I called around. I told them I wanted free med-

---

[1]Beginning on July 1, 1987, some disabled employees may be able to continue receiving a portion of SSI. To qualify, an individual must have monthly
income under $300–$400, and be incurring certain kinds of work-related
expenses.

ical care like at the county hospital, but I don't want to wait for twelve hours. The people said to try XYZ.[2] So I called there, and they said no one was waiting right then, so we went right away."

I sat holding the phone and grinning. Good old irrepressible, determined Nicole. I should have known she would figure out something.

"I like it there very, very much," she cooed, just before hanging up. "Whenever me and Edward have to see a doctor, we're going to go back there."

I replaced the receiver. XYZ Hospital was in a part of town where the thought of her and Edward walking to their car at night made me nervous, and the kind of care they would receive on future visits was an unknown—but she had found a solution for Edward's toe.

Resourcefulness. How could I have forgotten that commodity? I thought of how our informants in the UCLA research studies have *had* to become resourceful in order to get by on their modest incomes, to shop when they have difficulty reading signs and counting money, and to take care of the myriad other problems they encounter.

I remembered Ted Barrett, who has been followed by our researchers for over twenty years. His very survival in the skid-row section of Los Angeles, which he refuses to leave because his friends are there, is testimony to his resourcefulness.

And Irene Tucker, a black woman in her thirties who was so determined to become a meat wrapper that she went to the local library and had the librarian find and read a meat chart for her. When Irene had the meat cuts memorized, she hung around supermarket meat counters until someone finally agreed to train and

---

[2]XYZ is actually another county hospital.

hire her.[3]

Even Stanley Morris, a forty-year-old man who found an ingenious way to entertain before the days of video cassette rentals: he plugged in an old 16-mm movie projector and screened films borrowed from the public library like "Soil Erosion in the Farm Belt" for his popcorn-eating friends.

Yes, with time they do become resourceful. But resourcefulness doesn't always produce adequate medical care. It never pays taxes. It doesn't give parents solutions to fertility questions, and AIDS.

Was there no simple message for parents?

Gradually I realized that my message would have to be no. Parenting a mildly retarded adult during the move into independence is complicated. In the best of scenarios, we as parents struggle to make the right decisions, balancing our child's needs for self-determination against our concerns about his or her safety and wellbeing, as well as against our own needs as individuals.

We *do* need to be reminded about our children's need for self-determination. We too easily fall into the trap of imposing our values on their efforts to find happiness. At the same time, our children's very real incompetencies demand our involvement. We have to decide what we're going to do about their fertility, if anything, and how we will handle AIDS, and employment. Other things require decisions, too: should we allow them to borrow the camping equipment? Should we pick up the perishable groceries from a friend's house? Those kinds of decisions are often more wearing than the big ones.

---

[3]Koegel, P., & Edgerton, R. (1984). Black "six-hour retarded children" as young adults. In R. Edgerton (Ed.), *Lives in process: Mildly retarded adults in a large city*. Washington, DC: American Association on Mental Deficiency.

But I could express myself to parents simply and clearly about one matter: there is a legislative job to be done. Normalization is national policy. It mandates that retarded adults be integrated into the community as fully as possible—the ideal goal being an independent living arrangement and employment. Yet present policies not only are inconsistent with that goal, they undermine it.

I would remind parents of some history. During the early part of this century, most retarded persons were confined to residential hospitals. When deinstitutionalization began during the 1960s, the concept of normalization accompanied it. It is more humane, the authorities said. It was also cheaper. Millions of dollars were saved by emptying the state hospitals. Equivalent services were to be provided within the communities, we were told, and, indeed, in 1965 a bill establishing the Regional Center system was passed here in California.

Regional Center professionals are doing a critically important job in obtaining services for their adult clients. When it comes to health care, however, they have little to offer. For those clients who are eligible, there is Medi-Cal, the California version of Medicaid. But the inadequacies in the system are rife. Every step in the process is choked with paperwork, for patient as well as provider. Few physicians and hospitals accept Medi-Cal patients. Dental care is limited to extracting, not saving, teeth. Patients who need eyeglasses, hearing aids, and other appliances have to endure a nightmarish hassle obtaining them. Getting decent care under Medi-Cal is possible, but it demands time, patience, and, in many cases, luck.

For employed individuals with mental retardation, even this insurance has been ripped away. Medicaid originally provided coverage for the working poor, but eligibility was subsequently narrowed, and they are now excluded. As a result, wage earning retarded persons are now medically indigent, and Regional Center counselors refer them to the only places where the medically indigent are accepted, like the county hospitals. If eyeglasses or other appliances are needed, the patient either pays for them, or goes without.

Not only are retarded wage earners left without health care, they are punished with exorbitant taxation. Matt and I had hoped The Tax Reform Act of 1986 would provide some relief. It doesn't. In 1987 Nicole and Edward, and every other person like them, will be paying the same burdensome taxes.

These wrongs must be righted. All retarded individuals, even those who work and live independently, need help. All our retarded sons and daughters should have access to quality health care that is free, or available at minimal cost. It should be provided without demands that receipts be produced and forms completed, and it should be geographically accessible with a decent length of time in the waiting room. Eyeglasses, hearing aids, and similar aids should be obtainable under the same arrangements, as should decent dental care. When our legislators point out the expense entailed in providing such a health safety net, we should remind them of the millions of dollars that used to be spent each year institutionalizing these same retarded persons. Quality health insurance would cost a fraction of that.

As for taxation—it is a travesty that employed retarded persons are taxed at all. The loss of revenue incurred by removing them from the tax rolls would be miniscule.

President Kennedy said, "A nation is not to be judged by the strength of its arms, but by the way it cares for the least powerful of its citizens." Our legislators need to be reminded of these words.

Yes, that is what I will tell parents. Tomorrow I will get up early and continue writing.

And when I'm through, I'm going to write some long letters to my representatives in Congress.

Resources

The following books, articles, and educational documentary films are only a sampling of the works available on mental retardation. They have been selected with an eye toward introducing the reader to easily available ethnographic studies, that is, descriptive examinations of the lives of people with mental retardation. Books and articles that have been written for a professional audience are identified with a (P), but nonprofessionals should not cross them off. Anyone interested in a particular topic will find them quite interesting and accessible.

As an introduction to the entire field of research in mental retardation, I recommend:

Edgerton, R.B. (1979). *Mental retardation.* Cambridge: Harvard University Press.

Robert Edgerton has prepared a highly readable text that explains what is known about mental retardation and the questions this knowledge raises. The latter are what propel researchers to continue with their studies. The author's classification of "clinical" versus "sociocultural" retardation may perplex parents with children like Nicole whose retardation is mild yet was identified early in life, but the book contains a wealth of information.

Ethnographic Studies
of Mildly Mentally Retarded Adults

Edgerton, R.B. (1967). *The cloak of competence: Stigma in the lives of the Mentally Retarded.* Berkeley: University of California Press.

This is Edgerton's classic study in 1960–61 of forty-eight former residents of a California institution for the mentally deficient. (For a summary of the author's findings, see the Acknowledgments to this book on page xi.) (P)

Edgerton, R.B. (1981). Crime, deviance and normalization: Reconsidered. In R.H. Bruininks, C.E. Meyers, B.B. Sigford, & K.C. Lakin (Eds.), *Deinstitutionalization and community adjustment of mentally retarded people.* Monograph No. 4. Washington, DC: American Association on Mental Deficiency (1719 Kalorama Road, N.W., Washington, D.C. 20009).

Are mentally retarded persons more apt to commit crimes than nonretarded persons? The author examines the incidence of a crime and victimization among forty-eight mildly retarded informants over a two-and-a-half-year period. (P)

Edgerton, R.B. (Ed.) (1984). *Lives in process: Mildly retarded adults in a large city.* Monograph No. 6. Washington, DC: American Association on Mental Deficiency (1719 Kalorama Road, N.W., Washington, D.C. 20009).

Where do mildly retarded adults living independently find friends? Are they able to find stable employment? Do mildly retarded black children really blend into the general population once they leave school? These and other questions are explored by investigators engaged in long-term studies at the University of California, Los Angeles. (P)

Edgerton, R.B., & Bercovici, S. (1976). The cloak of competence: Years later. *American Journal of Mental Deficiency, 80,* 485–497.

Locating thirty of the original sample members, the authors revisited them twelve years later, and learned that their lives were no longer dominated by passing as normal and that Good Samaritans played a lesser role. Most of the subjects said they were as happy or happier than they had been in 1960. (P)

Edgerton, R., Bollinger, M., & Herr, B. (1984). The cloak of competence: After two decades. *American Journal of Mental Deficiency, 80,* 345–351.

Fifteen original sample members were recontacted. The authors found them even less dependent than before, and compared to aging mentally retarded persons described in other research reports, more hopeful and confident, despite ill health, stressful life events, and a lack of assistance from mental retardation service agencies. (P)

Turner, J.L. (1983). Workshop society: Ethnographic observations in a work setting for retarded adults. In K.T. Kernan, M.J. Begab, & R.B. Edgerton (Eds.), *Environments and behavior: The adaptation of mentally retarded persons* (pp. 147–172). Austin, TX: PRO-ED. (P)

Jim Turner and his research assistants spent over 9,000 hours in a sheltered workshop observing and interacting with the mentally retarded workers. In this article, Turner sums up what he has learned about the values, cultural rules, and concerns of this "workshop society." His findings may surprise a few sheltered workshop staff members. (P)

Turner, J.L., & Graffam, J. (1987, November). Deceased loved ones in the dreams of mentally retarded adults. *American Journal of Mental Deficiency, 92*(3), 282–289.

After listening to 154 dreams described by sheltered workshop clients, Turner and Graffam concluded that the dream life of mentally retarded adults is much more rich and diverse than suspected, and that deceased loved ones figure particularly heavily in it. Typical dreams are described, and implications are discussed for therapeutic work with retarded persons disturbed by nightmares. (P)

Zetlin, A., Turner, J., & Winik, L. (1987). Socialization effects on the adult adaptation of mildly retarded persons living in the community. In S. Landesman & P. Vietze (Eds.), *Living environments in mental retardation* (pp. 293–314). Washington, DC: American Association on Mental Retardation.

Is there any relationship between a retarded child's early socialization and his or her later success in living independently? After examining data gathered during long-term contact with thirty-seven mildly retarded adults, and conducting interviews with the parents, the authors conclude that there is. They describe three types of parent–child relationships—supportive, dependent, and conflict-ridden—and the kinds of community adaptation associated with each. (P)

Life Histories of
Persons with Mental Retardation:
In Their Own Voices

Bogdan, R., & Taylor, S.J. (1982). *Inside out: Two first person accounts of what it means to be labeled "mentally retarded."* Toronto: University of Toronto Press.

Personal histories of two former inmates of institutions for the retarded reveal the pain that labeling can inflict.

Hunt, N. (1967). *The world of Nigel Hunt: The diary of a mongoloid youth.* New York: Garrett.

Nigel Hunt, a child with Down syndrome who had a facility for language, was taught by his mother to read and write. In this remarkable diary, he describes his life in England, his travels, and his adjustment to his mother's death.

Langness, L., & Levine, H. (Eds.). (1986). *Culture and retardation: Life histories of mildly mentally retarded persons in American society.* Dordrecht, The Netherlands: D. Reidel Publishing Co.

Life history research methods are used to draw individual portraits of mildly retarded men and women. Each portrait explores how the human environment, particularly early family life and labeling, has affected the individual. (P)

Seagoe, M.V. (1964). *Yesterday was Tuesday, all day and all night: The story of a unique education.* Boston: Little, Brown.

Paul Scott, like Nigel Hunt, was a boy with Down syndrome who developed an unusual proficiency in expressing himself. The book consists principally of Scott's diary entries made during the years he traveled with his devoted father.

Turner, J. (1980). Yes I am human: Autobiography of a "retarded career." *Journal of Community Psychology, 8,* 3–8.

After spending two years interviewing Doug Valpey, a "mentally retarded" man, Turner gave him a battery of psychological tests and found he was of average intelligence. Turner discusses how Valpey, on learning of his changed status, revised his account of his life experiences. (P)

Marriage and Sexuality

Koegel, P., & Whittemore, R. (1983). Sexuality in the ongoing lives of mildly retarded adults. In A. Craft & M. Craft (Eds.), *Sex educa-*

tion and counseling for mentally handicapped people. Tunbridge Wells, England: Costello.

The authors, using Socio-Behavioral Research Group ethnographic data, describe widely ranging differences in forty-eight retarded informants' awareness of, and experience in, sex, as well as in their attitudes toward sex, marriage, birth control, and parenting. Included is a discussion of the serious psychological adjustment problems suffered by informants when pressured into abortions or sterilizations. Implications for counseling are outlined. (P)

Mattinson, J. (1971). *Marriage and mental handicap.* Pittsburgh: University of Pittsburgh Press.

For two years Mattinson studied thirty-two English married couples, both partners of which had come out of institutions for the mentally deficient. Mattinson related the happiness of the marriages to the low expectations the individuals had when they entered matrimony, and to the high degree of complementarity in the marital partnerships. By complementarity is meant the degree to which the individuals' dissimilarities balanced each other out. (P)

Parenting by Mentally Retarded Adults

Garber, H., & Heber, R. (1981). The efficacy of early intervention with family rehabilitation. In M. Begab, H.C. Haywood, & H.L. Garber (Eds)., *Psychosocial influences in retarded performance, Vol. II: Strategies for improving competence.* Baltimore: University Park Press.

The issue in this study was whether mental retardation can be prevented in children born into seriously disadvantaged homes. Eight years after an intervention program was established for mildly mentally retarded mothers and their infants living in an economically depressed area of Milwaukee, the authors were able to draw positive short-term conclusions. Concern remains about the outcome over time, however. (P)

Tucker, M.B., & Johnson, O. (in press, 1987). Competent promoting versus competent inhibiting social support for mentally retarded mothers. *Human Organization.*

Tucker and Johnson observed six black and six white mildly

mentally retarded mothers and their young children, all of whom were receiving extended support from family members or care providers. The authors conclude that support does not always encourage the learning of parenting skills; indeed, a helpful act may sometimes have negative consequences. Examples are presented, and the factors related to promoting competence are discussed. (P)

Zetlin, A., Weisner, T., & Gallimore, R. (1985). Diversity, shared functioning, and the role of benefactors: A study of parenting by retarded parents. In S.K. Thurman (Ed.), *Children of handicapped parents: Research and clinical perspectives* (pp. 69–96). Orlando, FL: Academic Press.

Thirteen retarded parents (three white, ten black) of preschool children were observed over a period of eighteen months. Most were perceived to be coping quite well as parents. Difficulties arose when the young mother had more than one child, or she lacked support from extended family members.   (P)

Educational Documentary Films

The Socio-Behavioral Research Group of the Mental Retardation Research Center, UCLA, has nine short films available for purchase. Subjects include the sheltered workshop studied by Jim Turner; Nicole and Edward's marriage; Ted Barrett's life in the skid row section of Los Angeles, and Doug Valpey who describes his feelings now that he realizes he is not retarded. Also available is a film of the five-hour symposium, "Coping with Community Life: Issues in the Everyday Lives of Mildly Retarded Adults," conducted at UCLA in April, 1984. Most of the films cost $50. For a complete listing, write to: SBG/NPI, Room 47-465, University of California, Los Angeles, 760 Westwood Plaza, Los Angeles, California 90024.

Of Special Help to Parents

Baladerian, N. (1987). *Survivor*. Manual available from The Los Angeles Commission on Assaults against Women, 543 North Fairfax Avenue, Los Angeles, California, 90036.

Survivor is a 78-page booklet full of drawings written for retarded individuals who have been sexually victimized or who are at risk for it. A companion volume is available for use by parents, care providers, and counselors.

Goldfarb, L., Brotherson, M.J., Summers, J.A., & Turnbull, A. (1986). *Meeting the challenge of disability or chronic illness—A family guide.* Baltimore: Paul H. Brookes Publishing Co.

  This is an ingeniously constructed manual for families who are feeling overwhelmed by the stress of coping with a mentally retarded, otherwise disabled, or chronically ill family member. Through step-by-step exercises, it helps readers clarify the problems they face, and become aware of the resources for solving them. A helpful bibliography is included.

Meyers, R. (1978). *Like normal people.* New York: McGraw-Hill Book Co.

  Robert Meyers, a journalist, has written a heart-warming account of his mildly retarded brother's move into independence and subsequent marriage. Skillfully woven through the story is a history of society's responses to mental retardation, particularly over the last century.

Murphy, A.T. (1981). *Special children, special parents: Personal issues with handicapped children.* Englewood Cliffs, NJ: Prentice-Hall.

  Albert Murphy, who is Professor of Special Education, Communication Disorders, and Rehabilitation Medicine at Boston University, is a clinical psychologist. Frequently quoting the words of parents themselves, he has written an encouraging, helpful book for parents of all kinds of handicapped children.

Useful Addresses for Parents

  Only a few of the many national organizations that provide services to families with disabled members are listed here. Other organizations address the concerns of specific disabilities. Consult your library, agencies in your state, and these organizations for more information on other services.

American Association on Mental Retardation, 1719 Kalorama Road, N.W., Washington, DC 20009

Association for Retarded Citizens of the United States, 2501 Avenue J, Arlington, Texas 76011

Closer Look, Parents' Campaign for Handicapped Children and Youth, 1201 16th Street, N.W., Washington, DC 20036

Council for Exceptional Children, 1920 Association Drive, Reston, Virginia 22091

National Information Center for Handicapped Children and Youth, P.O. Box 1492, Washington, DC 20013

The Sibling Information Network, Department of Educational Psychology, Box U-64, The University of Connecticut, Storrs, Connecticut 06268

An Afterword

The parents of children with mental retardation usually face many difficult decisions. When the child does not develop as rapidly as other children, how do parents find professional help? How do they know whether the help they obtain is appropriate and not high-priced quackery? How do they deal with the expectations and rejection of teachers and schoolmates, of neighborhood children or adults? How do they explain to their intellectually normal children that their retarded sibling cannot learn as quickly or as well as they do? As the child grows into puberty, how do they protect him or her from the pain that can be so much a part of adolescence, of sexual experimentation, of rebellion and risk-taking? And how do they cope when their child insists on leaving home?

Sandra Kaufman and her husband grappled with all of these problems—and more. But it is important to realize that what they did for their daughter Nicole and how they felt about her are hardly unique. Their fears and doubts are shared by most parents of mildly retarded children. It is because their experience with Nicole was so typical—I hesitate to say commonplace, for I do not mean to diminish the heartaches

227

that they and others like them endured—that this book is so powerful. What they suffered is what most parents suffer. The illusion of hope that there could be a medical "cure" was shattered by the discovery of quackery. The frustrating search for knowledge about Nicole's condition and her future prospects led to insensitive professionals who made Sandra feel guilty for her daughter's failures. When Nicole asks what "retard" means, the explanation to her and to her siblings will sound familiar to many parents, familiar but so difficult and so painful. Nicole's academic failures will be all too familiar to parents as well, and so will her indomitable spirit, although readers who are not acquainted with persons who have mental retardation may be surprised by this latter quality.

The core of the book is devoted to Nicole's decision to leave her parents' home. Although memory can play tricks about such things, this was perhaps the greatest challenge for Nicole's parents, and surely it is a lasting one. It was challenging for all the mundane reasons having to do with responsible housekeeping, cooking, and budgeting, but especially because Nicole was determined to live with her boyfriend Edward, and she was not prepared to use birth control methods. She wanted a baby. But now the story changes. There was no disaster. Nicole and Edward were married, learned to cope with the everyday problems of life, and there was no baby. To be sure, they coped as well as they did in part because Nicole's parents offered all kinds of support, including money when it was needed. But over the years their ability to rely on their own skills and resources grew, just as it usually does. The early period of adjustment to independent living is almost always troubled, and life, for parents and children alike, can resemble a runaway roller-coaster ride. However, with support and time to adjust, most mildly and even moderately retarded people (people with IQs from roughly 40 to 70) can make a good adaptation to life on their own.

Sandra Kaufman's account of this process of adaptation is extraordinarily vivid and moving. Readers will not only understand what Nicole and her parents went through, they will feel it. That is so in large measure because this book is so well written, but it is also so because Sandra Kaufman achieved what was very nearly impossible by stepping out of her role as a mother caught up in years-old relationships of mistrust, dependency, frustration, and love, into a new role of objective observer of Nicole and her life including her relationship with her mother. On the face of it, Sandra's transformation from a passionately involved mother into a distant, unbiased outsider is so unlikely that readers may wonder if such a change really took place. They have every reason to be skeptical. Anthropologists, who pioneered the methods she used, have long known how difficult it is to "study" people with whom one identifies or to whom one is emotionally attached, but Sandra Kaufman learned her craft well (from mentors wiser than I) and she employed her skills judiciously. The result is a convincing portrayal of how very different Nicole appears as a person once her world is seen through her own eyes. There is no pretense here that the author has put all of her feelings as a mother behind her—far from it; but the evidence clearly shows that she has been remarkably successful in seeing things as Nicole does.

There is an important issue here. For many years, professionals in the field of mental retardation have, on the one hand, believed that many parents restrict their children's opportunities for normal experience by holding them in tenacious dependency relationships. Parents, on the other hand, often argue that this criticism by professionals is unjust, insisting that they know better than any outsider what their child is capable of and that without their support and love their children would lead barren, miserable lives. There is truth on both sides of this argument. Many parents, perhaps even most parents, do restrict their children's lives and subtly encourage the development of dependency. Parents also, however, are very often the best, most compassionate and reliable source of affection and support for their retarded children, not only while they are still at home, but after they move out as well. Sandra Kaufman's book will not resolve this Janus-faced dilemma of parents and their children, but it will help professionals to better understand parents' perspectives and it may help parents to see themselves and their children more clearly. It is also not too much to hope that it will help some mentally retarded persons to understand their parents a little better. Anyone with an interest in mental retardation can learn from this sensitive and loving book.

Robert B. Edgerton, Ph.D.
Socio-Behavioral Research Group
Mental Retardation Research Center
University of California–Los Angeles

Postscript
June 1991

Three years have passed since *Retarded Isn't Stupid, Mom!* was first published. Some things remain the same. Nicole and Edward are childless. They are employed, although each is now at a different place of business. Friends and social occasions play a large part in their lives. Matt and I underwrite their rent.

But changes have occurred. The much loved nephews have moved to Tennessee. Nicole and Edward now have medical insurance through the restaurants where they work.

They no longer own a car. A year and a half ago someone side-swiped the Datsun in a parking lot. Shortly after having it repaired, Nicole drove out from behind a STOP sign at a blind corner and hit a slowly moving car. No one was injured and the vehicular damage looked minimal, but their insurance company declared the Datsun not worth saving. Nicole was handed a check for $1,600.

Since then they have depended on their mopeds and public transportation to get around. It is an imperfect solution. Last summer a driver, failing to see Nicole on her moped, ducked in front of her. Nicole was thrown and knocked unconscious. Luckily she had a helmet on, and her only injuries were a sprained ankle and contusions. A few months later another driver cut her off, causing her to swerve and tumble to avoid a collision. She scolded the driver—I'm sure he'll never forget the tongue lashing—but she was unhurt. After these two incidents she is riding buses more often now.

Matt and I did not step in to subsidize a new car. It was time to back away from that kind of help. Besides, they could afford one themselves, what with the $1,600 settlement, royalties from the sale of this book, and $300 a month from a second trust deed. We did become involved, though, when we discovered that none of this bounty was being saved.

It took a few sessions for the four of us to figure out a system by which they could keep track of what they were spending, but the program was soon working better than any of us expected. Matt and I now merely show up once a week and watch while they sort through the previous week's receipts and Edward records them in ledger columns. They like doing it. Money is no longer something that provides goodies and then capriciously vanishes. The two of them see it come in and go out for commodities like movies, video rentals, telephone bills, and presents for the nephews. Empowered by this knowledge, Nicole and Edward have altered their habits and are saving money—with gratifying results. This Sunday they will rent a car and leave for a week's vacation in a mountain resort (with Shelley in tow), something they were unable to do before.

In sum, they continue to learn. We remain involved, and if we are out of town, David or Jill are there. Lest the picture appear too rosy, let me add that problems remain. Nicole's weight is the principal one. It has worried us for years, but until now she has resisted changes in her eating and cooking habits. The recent discovery that her blood pressure is high has motivated her to make alterations. Whether she can master the knowledge her doctor and I are providing (it must be memorized because she has such difficulty reading) and has the willpower to diet are still open questions. All we can say now is that she is interested and trying.

Matt's and my relationship with Nicole and Edward isn't one-way. When we are vacationing, they live in our house. On our return Matt and I always find the mail neatly stacked, the plants green, and the sheets on our bed fresh. Of course, a few parties have occurred during the occupancy. Some things never change. Nicole has always seen the possibilities in a situation and taken advantage of them.